My
Sunday
Best

My Sunday Best

PEARLS OF WISDOM, WIT, GRACE, AND STYLE

Dr. La Verne Ford Wimberly

with Barbranda Lumpkins Walls

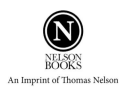

NELSON
BOOKS

An Imprint of Thomas Nelson

To my parents, Jesse Eugene Ford and Clydie Vernice Smith Ford; my husband, James Oliver Wimberly; and sister, Jewell Vernice Maynard, for their enduring encouragement, love, and support. Thanks for helping me soar. I am eternally grateful.

Contents

Who would
have thought

that an
eighty-two-year-old
Black lady wearing
her Sunday best
would go

VIRAL?

SELFIE 1

MARCH 29, 2020

MY SUNDAY BEST: For my first selfie I put on a wide-brim, frilly white hat; a simple white blouse with eyelet inserts; a turquoise skirt; and matching turquoise jewelry.

Introduction

It all started
with the pandemic.

I never miss going to church on Sunday.

So, on March 29, 2020, the first Sunday that my beloved Metropolitan Baptist Church in Tulsa had a virtual worship service because of the pandemic, I knew that giving honor and glory to God in my bathrobe or workout gear was *not* an option.

I was raised to present myself to the Lord wearing my very best. At eighty-two years old, I couldn't start being a slouch before God, even though I was alone at home. So, just like any other Sunday, I got up and got dressed. The song "Brighten the Corner Where You Are" that I learned in church when I was a child came to mind. It's still one of my favorites today. The words resonate with me, and maybe with you too:

Brighten the Corner Where You Are

Do not wait until some deed of greatness you may do,
Do not wait to shed your light afar;
To the many duties ever near you now be true,
Brighten the corner where you are.

Refrain:
Brighten the corner where you are!
Brighten the corner where you are!
Someone far from harbor you may guide across the bar;
Brighten the corner where you are!

Just above the clouded skies that you may help to clear,
Let not narrow self your way debar;
Though into one heart alone may fall your song of cheer,
Brighten the corner where you are.

Here for all your talent you may surely find a need,
Here reflect the bright and Morning Star;
Even from your humble hand the Bread of Life may feed,
Brighten the corner where you are.

With that song running through my mind,

I put on a wide-brim, frilly white hat; a simple white blouse with eyelet inserts; a turquoise skirt; and matching turquoise jewelry. I'm usually more formally attired for an in-person service, but I thought it would be fun to snap a selfie and post it on Facebook. I let folks know that I was ready to worship and encouraged them to do the same. Some of my fellow church members are Facebook friends, and this was my way to brighten their spirits—and mine—and stay connected during a time of sudden isolation and despair for many people.

After posting that first selfie, I kept doing it. Week after week I got up on Sunday morning and put on a different outfit and a different hat and snapped a photo of myself. In the ninth week I started to add a scripture or inspirational message. I never imagined that more than a year would go by before my church resumed in-person services. For fifty-two consecutive Sundays, I posted a picture of myself on Facebook—dressed in my Sunday best—and I never repeated a hat or an outfit!

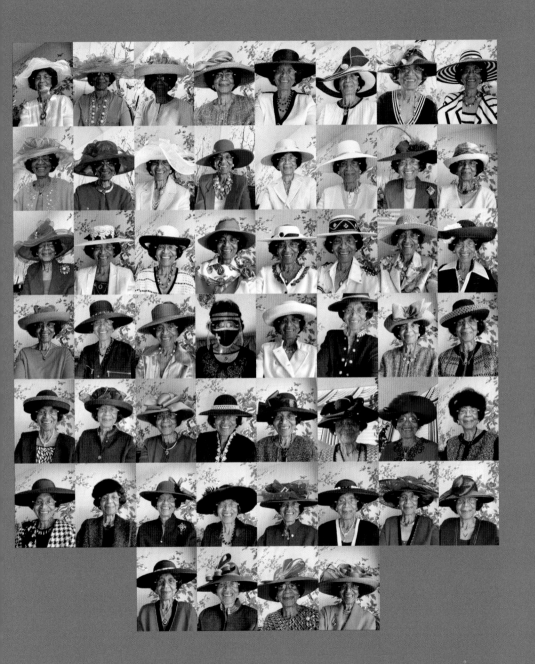

After fifty-two weeks,

our church had its last virtual worship service and, on March 21, 2021, I posted my final Sunday Selfie. Kim Jackson, a reporter for Tulsa's KTUL ABC channel 8, is a member of Metropolitan and saw my post. Several times before, Kim had asked to interview me about my career as an educator, and I'd always said no. This time, I said yes and agreed to do a Zoom interview.

The mainstream media caught wind of it, and the response was overwhelming. Some outlets mentioned me, and others interviewed me.

Here are some of the places I appeared.

Anderson Cooper's
Full Circle on CNN

Fox News

The Washington Post

Tulsa World

ABC News

MSNBC

CBS News

Today Show

Trevor Noah

Dan Rather even mentioned me on Twitter!

People from all over the world have said my selfies and words of encouragement have blessed and inspired them.

Then the gifts started to arrive. Here are some of the wonderful presents I received!

Jen Hager, from New Jersey, painted my selfies on several jean jackets. She did a marvelous job! Thanks again, Jen!

Jen Hager is at **Northeastern University**. ...
Oct 23, 2021 · Boston, MA 👥

La Verne Ford Wimberly I'm wearing your jacket! I get so many compliments because they all know you and want to hear about your outfits!! 🖤🖤🤍 🤍🖤🖤🖤

A retailer called Especially Yours sent me this lovely yellow suit and hat.

I was delighted to receive this hat and purple suit from the Ashro Company.

I got this lovely hat from the
Meshugenah Hat Company
in Troy, New Hampshire.

An unidentified person
from Illinois sent me
this stunning hat.

A teacher named S. Mason from
Mitchellville, Maryland, made
me this unique memory game.

Someone even created a puzzle!
This is the cover.

A special thank you to Winifred Creamer from Pacific Grove, Ca. She made this beautiful beach glass necklace for me. I deeply appreciate her goodwill and generosity! It matches my blouse perfectly. Love it!

A special thank you to my childhood friend, Marilyn Britton Mayes from Chicago, IL and her son, Ernie Mayes. Ernie made me a DVD with several of the media interviews shown around the world. I especially love the jacket that encases the DVD including the inscriptions. I genuinely appreciate it! Another lifetime keepsake! Love it!

La Verne Ford Wimberly

⭐ Favorites · May 12, 2021 · 👥

The gifts keep coming. A special thank you to Lisa German from San Antonio, Texas. She sent me glassware with my pictures on them and two trivets/coasters. She is my Soror and she monogrammed my name on a towel. I love them.

This is one of six 8x10 acrylic paintings that I received from Kerry Maeder in Albuquerque, New Mexico. All six paintings are displayed proudly on my hearth!

I never imagined

my Sunday Best selfies would stir up such love from total strangers! A couple from New York sent me $5o! How about that?

I am supremely grateful for each gift!

I awoke this morning with devout thanksgiving for my friends, the old and the new.

—Ralph Waldo Emerson

Then someone called and asked
if I wanted to do a book.

My motto is:

Think Before You Act.

That was written on a plaque hanging on the chalkboard in every single classroom at my alma mater, George Washington Carver Junior High.

I still adhere to that motto.

I take my time before acting on something. I think about the consequences and ramifications of my actions. As my mother used to say, "He who acts as his own attorney has a fool for a client."

I took my time and thought about writing a book.

Eventually I said yes because God has allowed me to live **a glorious life!**

I never dreamed
I'd do a book

but I'm a natural encourager
and hope I can encourage you
and brighten the corner
where you are.

SELFIE 2

APRIL 5, 2020

MY SUNDAY BEST: I would never wear a casual top like this to an in-person Sunday service, so I paired it with a wide-brim, off-the-rack, frilly, over-the-top hat and several necklaces to create a dressier look!

My childhood silhouette.

Wisdom, Wit, Grace, and Style

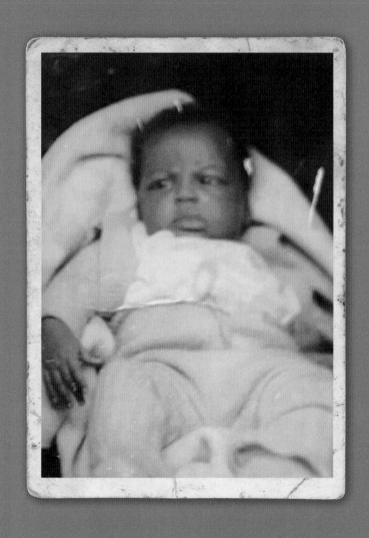

Home

I come from humble beginnings. I was born in Tulsa, Oklahoma, on January 29, 1939, to the best parents this side of heaven. My dad, Jesse Eugene Ford, and mom, Clydie Smith Ford, were my first examples of strength, courage, resourcefulness, and godliness. They also gave my older sister, Jewell, and me a strong foundation of faith. Dad and Mother were loving, but they had high expectations for us. Jewell and I strived to please them and make them proud.

My father was a mechanic who suffered a debilitating stroke in his forties and couldn't work after that. My mother, a domestic worker for a wealthy white family in Tulsa, picked

3

up the slack. Not only did Mother go to work every day, she also took great care of my dad, my sister, and me—and did so without complaint. Mother could stretch a dollar like nobody's business and never missed any event or activity that involved Jewell and me.

I had an idyllic childhood. Yes, it was that good. We were poor, but I didn't know it. I grew up in Tulsa's Greenwood District, home of the renowned Black Wall Street, with its many Black-owned and operated businesses. We had everything we needed within walking distance—stores, cleaners, pharmacies, hair salons, barbershops, restaurants, movie theaters, doctors, dentists, and churches. That community was like a family. They stepped up and filled in the gap, especially when my father was ill and couldn't do the things that other fathers did for their children. Teachers and neighbors escorted my sister and me to events like father-daughter banquets. We had that village support—a nucleus who wrapped their arms around us.

We looked out for each other.

SELFIE 3

APRIL 12, 2020

MY SUNDAY BEST: Since it was Easter Sunday, I thought I needed to look spiffier than I had the previous two weeks, so I donned my pink suit with the sequin trim and topped off the look with my pink floral hat.

Greenwood District, Black Wall Street

I am proud of who I am and where I come from: the historic Greenwood District in Tulsa, Oklahoma, also known as Black Wall Street. In the 1900s, the Greenwood District was developing into what became North America's most prosperous African American community. Sadly, the neighborhood was primarily destroyed by a race riot May 31–June 1, 1921. Known as the Tulsa Race Massacre, seventy-five to three hundred African Americans were killed, two thousand businesses were destroyed, and ten thousand people became homeless (Greenwood Cultural Center website). Several years later, the neighborhood was rebuilt, and the seeds of entrepreneurship, community, faith, and family remained vital for decades. I knew families who worked hard to build businesses on Tulsa's Black Wall Street in the 30s, 40s, and 50s. They wanted to leave a legacy for their children and grandchildren. But urban renewal came through in the 1960s and 70s and wiped out most of the Black businesses. Some people tried to rebuild, but so many who came from the families of those original entrepreneurs didn't have the drive or desire to follow in their ancestors' footsteps.

I am the chairperson of the Board of Directors of the Greenwood Cultural Center (GCC). In 2021, we commemorated the 100th anniversary of the massacre with various ceremonies and events that included the three known survivors and various government officials and celebrities.

Youngsters must know their history and carry on the legacy. Knowing the history of how we overcame as a people and how we made it through difficult times needs to be emphasized, especially to the younger generation.

In life, we have to press on despite obstacles and keep going. When I was at Carver Junior High, my teacher, Mrs. M. O. Williams, read us a poem called *"Keep A-Goin'!"* by Frank Stanton and encouraged us to memorize it. That poem made such an impact on me that, after I became a teacher, I hung it on the wall of all my classrooms. By God's grace and with His help, we must keep going.

I'm inspired by these centenarians—the three known survivors of the Tulsa Race Massacre, 1921: Viola Fletcher (108), Hughes Van Ellis (101) and Lessie Benningfield Randle (107).

Upper left: Booker T. Washington high school parade on Greenwood Avenue, 1930s or 1940s. (Courtesy of the Greenwood Cultural Center.)

Upper right: Circa early twentieth century. A cinema and stage theater, the Dreamland, was destroyed during the Tulsa Race Massacre, in 1921. (Courtesy of the Greenwood Cultural Center.)

Lower left: Greenwood Avenue in the 1940s, when I was a little girl. (Courtesy of the Greenwood Cultural Center.)

Lower right: The Harris Prescription Laboratory in the 1940s or 1950s. I worked there in the late 1950s and early 1960s. (Courtesy of the Greenwood Cultural Center.)

"Keep A-Goin'!"

Ef you strike a thorn or rose,
Keep a-goin'!
Ef it hails, or ef it snows,
Keep a-goin'!
'Taint no use to sit an' whine,
When the fish ain't on yer line;
Bait yer hook an' keep a-tryin—
Keep a-goin'!

When the weather kills yer crop,
Keep a-goin'!
When you tumble from the top,
Keep a-goin'!
S'pose you're out o' every dime,
Bein' so ain't any *crime*;
Tell the world you're feelin' *prime*—
Keep a-goin'!

When it looks like all is up,
Keep a-goin'!
Drain the sweetness from the cup,
Keep a-goin'!
See the wild birds on the wing,
Hear the bells that sweetly ring,
When you feel like sighin' sing—
Keep a-goin'!

—FRANK LEBBY STANTON (1900) PUBLIC DOMAIN

SELFIE 4
APRIL 19, 2020

MY SUNDAY BEST: By week four, I started to get back into my formal church fashion, so I put on a suit that I love. I have about sixty hats but this one is my second favorite. I love the way the material swirls around the brim. Isn't it stunning?

Worship

Come, let us bow down in worship, let
us kneel before the Lord our Maker.

—PSALM 95:6 NIV

Since early childhood, worshiping on Sunday has been a major part of my life. I subscribe to Proverbs 22:6 that says, "Train up a child in the way he should go: and when he is old, he will not depart from it" (KJV). My parents made sure we were grounded in our Christian faith. We attended Union Baptist Church, where I started to learn all about worshiping the Lord. I am now a member of Metropolitan Baptist Church, where I serve as chairwoman of the board of trustees.

I grew up in the church and I never strayed from it. For years when I traveled, I looked for a Sunday worship service wherever I was—even in airports. I just felt something wasn't right unless I had that weekly worship experience. One of the most memorable worship experiences I had was when I visited the Holy Land in 2014. I had a deep sense that Jesus was right there with me at the Garden Tomb, the site of His burial and resurrection. Oh, what a feeling that was!

I had never missed a Sunday in church—until COVID-19 swept in and shut down most places of worship. But as you know, even a pandemic didn't stop me from worshiping God. My family room or office became my makeshift sanctuary as I sat alone, dressed in my Sunday best, with my laptop to tune in to the online services.

I was overjoyed to return to in-person worship at Metropolitan Baptist after a year! I sat in my usual spot, the last row in section two, seat one, surrounded by my church family. I was right back where I belonged, worshiping the Lord in spirit and in truth.

Gracious God, may my worship of You be acceptable in Your sight. You are truly worthy of all praise. In Jesus' name. Amen.

Blessed are the clean of heart, for they will see God

The
BEST
IS YET
TO COME
if you
PREPARE
for it.

SELFIE 5

APRIL 26, 2020

MY SUNDAY BEST: This is my all-time favorite hat, because I designed it at a milliner's shop in Louisiana about thirty years ago. I cherish my hats so much! I keep them in huge hat boxes with tissue, so this hat still looks new!

Teaching

I was blessed to have a long and successful career as an educator. Before I retired in 2006 from the Tulsa Public Schools as assistant superintendent for public schools of choice and family ombudsman services, I spent more than forty years as a teacher, guidance counselor, principal, administrator, and interim superintendent. It was a path that I sort of stumbled into.

I studied psychology at the University of Tulsa with plans to become a clinical psychologist. But I soon found out that I couldn't do anything with my bachelor's degree without a master's degree. A childhood friend who was teaching in

Chicago told me her school system was looking for teachers and I could get a job there. Just as she said, I applied and was soon hired. My first assignment was teaching first graders. I just fell in love with those little darlings. I remained in education and never looked back.

I believe teaching is a calling. You must be prepared to do it right and have lots of compassion. And you must treat everyone—students, parents, and colleagues—with dignity and respect. I enjoyed teaching because I loved helping my students acquire new skills and knowledge that would help them become successful. I was blessed with some wonderful teachers when I was growing up. They inspired and encouraged me in so many ways. One in particular, Ione Wright Morrison, was my high school speech teacher. She knew her subject matter and wanted her students to speak correctly. She was no nonsense, yet gentle and kind. I wanted to please Mrs. Morrison and all my teachers. Just call me a teacher pleaser.

When I was young, I had other plans for my life, which included being an airline stewardess so that I could travel the world. But I believe it was God's will for me to teach. He allowed me to touch so many lives and have a lasting impact. I couldn't ask for anything more.

Dear Lord, thank You for helping me to fulfill Your purpose and using me to be a positive influence on others. Help me to not only teach but to learn. In Jesus' name. Amen.

LEARNING

is an

ONGOING

pursuit.

SELFIE 6

MAY 3, 2020

MY SUNDAY BEST: About ten years ago, I was shopping for church hats when I saw this one. I *had* to have it because it was covered with bling, plus I needed a blue-and-white hat to match an outfit.

Elegant

Strength and dignity are her clothing,
And she smiles at the future.

—PROVERBS 31:25 NASB

I got my sense of style from my mother. And my teachers at Carver Junior High made a huge impression on me. They were so elegant and fashionably dressed every single day in their circle skirts and matching sweater twin sets. Versie Dale Alford, my typing teacher, had a twin set in every color: lavender, fuchsia, yellow, blue, and more. Helena Freeman and Inez Stubblefield Black were the same. I still remember the names of these teachers and how they looked. These women were always dressed to the nines in their skirts and heels, with their nails done and not a strand of hair out of place.

My high school teachers kept up the tradition. I thought then that when I grew up and had a job, I wanted to look like them every day. And I did. As a teacher, I walked into the classroom each day impeccably dressed. I thought that was so important. I wanted to be an example to the children and to teach them to take pride in their appearance. They used to tell me, "Oh, Miss Ford, you look so pretty." They noticed.

Sadly, so many teachers today

don't care how they look and go to work any old kind of way. I believe if you look your best, you do your best.

During the pandemic, while I was dressing in my Sunday best each week, I kept a calendar of what I wore so that I wouldn't repeat outfits. I kept my first calendar of outfits in Chicago when I started teaching. I didn't want to duplicate a look in the week or the month. Vanity, oh, vanity!

While appearance is important, I know it's not the only thing that matters. In 1 Samuel 16:7, the Lord essentially tells the prophet Samuel, "The LORD does not look at the things people look at. People look at the outward appearance, but the LORD looks at the heart."

What's in your heart matters most of all. A heart filled with love, compassion, and grace is better than any beautiful or elegant garment.

Dear Lord, please clothe me in Your strength, dignity, and righteousness so that I may present myself well and bring glory to You. Amen.

SELFIE 7

MAY 10, 2020

MY SUNDAY BEST: This is my third favorite hat. I love black-and-white hats for summer, and this one has a bit of yellow to make it pop!

Crown

Now there is in store for me the crown
of righteousness, which the Lord, the
righteous Judge, will award to me on that
day—and not only to me, but also to all
who have longed for his appearing.

—2 TIMOTHY 4:8 NIV

My love of hats was inspired by my mother. She always wore one to church, which is a tradition among many Black women, especially in the Baptist church. We call those "church hats" our crowns, and we proudly wear them to Sunday worship.

I have nearly sixty hats in three, bedroom closets. I have them stored in big hat boxes, labeled by color. I was twenty-two when I started collecting hats in 1963 while I was living in Chicago. I bought my first fancy one in New Orleans. I was in the French Quarter and saw a hat shop called Fleur de Paris. I decided to treat myself and have a hat made just for me. I described what I wanted: a black, wide brim, straw hat with a veil. It's still my favorite. Another one I love is a gray straw hat adorned with gray fabric. It fits my head perfectly. It's like one of those big, fancy hats you see women wear at the Kentucky Derby.

After that I started buying hats in various places during my travels. I'm a fan of wide brim hats that I can bend to my liking. I usually wear them tilted to the right. You have to find a style you like and stick with it. I also love to color-coordinate them with my outfits.

I'm a bling girl. I've always been

fascinated by gold and glitter. You have any of that going on and you have my attention.

But the crown I really want and am working toward is the crown of righteousness. I will receive that from the Lord after I leave this world and enter into eternity with Jesus. I don't fear or mind dying. I know death is inevitable. I'm just not ready to go yet. There are so many places I want to see. And I want to see my great-nephews grow up because I've invested so much in them. I want to see them establish their relationship with the Lord.

It's hard to imagine what heaven will be like. I can't seem to visualize something that surpasses the beauty I've seen here on earth. John's vision of heaven in the book of Revelation talks about streets paved with gold and each of the twelve gates made of a single pearl. There is no sickness or disease, no cloudy days in heaven. It is a place that is peaceful and endearing. Will we walk around in heaven all day wearing a real crown? I'm not sure. But being in such a place, fully in God's presence, will be my crown.

Heavenly Father, thank You for the promise of a crown of righteousness when I see You face-to-face. May I always keep heaven in view as I await Your return. In Jesus' name. Amen.

MY SUNDAY BEST: I like this suit because of the variation in the black and white stripes; some stripes are horizontal, and some are diagonal. When I saw this hat, I had to purchase it, because I knew it would go perfectly with this outfit!

Take on the

MINDSET

of ACHIEVEMENT and

WINNING.

Love and Marriage

*Love does not delight in evil but rejoices
with the truth. It always protects, always
trusts, always hopes, always perseveres.*

—1 CORINTHIANS 13:6–7 NIV

**Everybody needs love and
affection**—to feel wanted and a
sense of belonging. If I expect to be
loved, I have to give love. **Love is
a give-and-take.** It goes back and
forth. With love there has to be compromise between individuals.

I met James Oliver Wimberly
when I was a young teen. Someone
had broken into our home and stolen the costume jewelry that my
sister had received as gifts for her
high school graduation. James was
the police officer who answered the
call. Our paths didn't cross again
until I was in college and working at
a pharmacy in Tulsa. He was writing
parking tickets for cars of our customers who stopped to pick up their
medications. I had the nerve to tell
him he needed to stop doing that.
Then, years later, we met again at
a party and hit it off. We got married on March 11, 1965, when I was
twenty-six. James was considerably
older than I was. In fact, he'd been
married before and had two children,
Ann and Mark.

James and I had an unconventional wedding. After dating for nearly two years, we eloped. One night James told me that it was time for us to get married and I simply said, "Okay." So, the next day he picked me up during my lunch hour from my job in customer service at the Tulsa Water Department—the first African American to work in that department—and we drove about twenty-five miles in the pouring rain to the courthouse in Sapulpa, Oklahoma, to tie the knot.

The justice of the peace there was about a thousand years old and could barely recite the marriage vows because he was trembling so much. But we made it through the quick ceremony, got back in the car, and returned to Tulsa. James dropped me off at work and he returned to his shift as a police officer. At the end of our workday, he picked me up again and took me to my parents' house, and he went to his aunt's house where he lived at the time.

When I told my parents that I had gotten married, they didn't believe me. Mother asked for evidence. I showed her the marriage certificate and that was that. No fuss, no muss, no congratulations. If Mother was upset or disappointed, she never said so. I continued to live with Mother and Daddy for two weeks until James and I bought our first home just outside of the Greenwood District. We lived there for seven years.

James was from the old school. He believed he was the man of the house and that I should show respect to him. And I did. He also respected me. As I said, love is a give-and-take and is reciprocal. James and I had a loving relationship for more than four decades, up until the day he died.

While I cherished James's love, I always knew God's love was something even more special. I grew up hearing that God is love. I know without a doubt that He loves me.

While I can never repay the Lord for His love, I try to show my love for Him by loving Him and by loving my neighbor and myself.

Heavenly Father, thank You for the love of family and friends. But most of all, thank You for first loving me. In Jesus' name I pray. Amen.

SELFIE 9

MAY 24, 2020

MY SUNDAY BEST: This lavender hat caught my eye because of the color but also because of the gray metallic trim that is on the edge of the bows, and it blends in nicely with my lavender twin sweater set. By now, you know that I love bling, so of course, there's some bling on this outfit as well!

Give thanks to the LORD, for he is good;
his love endures forever.

—PSALM 107:1 NIV

I'm grateful for so many things in my life! A loving family. Long-lasting friendships. A successful career. Good health and strength. The desire and ability to serve others. A close walk with Jesus. And while it might sound strange, there is one thing I am particularly grateful for—how my husband, James, died.

James had faced some earlier health issues (he had beaten both prostate and bladder cancer), but his death on October 27, 2009, was totally unexpected. He had been doing fine. Earlier that week, he had enjoyed breakfast at his favorite restaurant, savored his favorite snack of some buttermilk and Twinkies that a friend had brought to him, and I had prepared two of his favorite dishes—stuffed peppers and vegetable soup. The evening before God called him home, James kept staring at me while we sat together and watched *Dancing with the Stars* on TV. When I asked him why he was looking at me that way, he said, "I just wanted to stare at my beautiful wife." I smiled and told him to carry on.

The next morning, as I prepared breakfast, James called to me from the back room and asked for the Snuggie blanket with sleeves that he liked to use when he was chilly. I put it over him, and as I walked away, I heard him gasp. For years, James loved to pretend he was dying to try to get a rise out of me. He never succeeded. But this time when I turned around and looked at him, I knew it was different. He didn't respond when I called his name several times. I dialed 911 and administered CPR. But he had already left here, peacefully. Just like that. As far as I'm concerned, that's the way to go.

James had always said he wanted to die before me because he did not want me to leave him here on this earth alone. So that's why I am grateful. The Lord knew the wishes of James's heart and granted him the privilege of passing away in his own home with me nearby. I thank God for that—and so much more.

In the early 1960s when I was about twenty-one years old, I went to Woods Photography Studio and had a sepia-tone portrait made of myself. James absolutely loved that photo. He kept it on our bedroom dresser and would speak to it every day. "Hello, how are you doing today?" he would sometimes say as he passed by. He always acknowledged that photograph. James often told me that he would pass away before me, and he requested that picture be buried with him. I never would have thought to do such a thing. But I honored his wishes at the end. I put a framed copy of the portrait in his casket. Here it is.

I was attracted to James Oliver Wimberly because he was kind, mature, had a decent job, and was tall at six foot two. (Three inches taller than I was!) And he was fascinated with me. He thought I was smart and had the potential to do great things. He saw that in me before I did. James was the one who encouraged me to return to school and get a master's degree and to pursue administrative positions in education. He also thought I was a know-it-all, but in a good way. He later wanted me to go to law school and become an attorney because I spoke well and was persuasive. He used to call me "Ms. E. F. Hutton," saying when I talked, people listened.

James was my biggest supporter and cheerleader.

On page 38 is one my favorite photos of James. Wasn't he handsome?

James dropped out of high school to join the navy so that he would have money to help his older sister go to Langston University. After a stint in the navy, he returned to Tulsa and finished high school. He saw there was a need for police officers and became one. He also sometimes worked an extra job as a security guard. He was on the police force for thirty-two years before he retired.

My husband was an avid reader. He could talk to anybody very intelligently on almost any subject. He

was that well-read. He especially liked *National Geographic* and science. I gave away more than five hundred books to the library after he died. He especially liked to browse through recipe books and then try to tell me what I needed to be cooking. He cooked a little too. His signature dish was a one-skillet combo of sausage, cabbage, Irish potatoes, green peppers, tomatoes, and onions. With a piece of cornbread, that was a good meal. And I got the night off from cooking.

James grew up on a farm and was a very good gardener. He had a garden at our home and grew mustard greens, tomatoes, green beans, okra, squash, and green peppers. He would get so aggravated with me when he brought in tomatoes and other fresh vegetables, and I didn't do something with them that very day. But I did love the okra and I would fry that for us. One morning I fried fifty pods at one time and snacked on okra throughout the day. I do miss his okra and his mustard greens. In fact, I still LOVE

fried okra and eat it like popcorn! My family and friends know that I love okra and give me bags of it as gifts! If we're in a restaurant and okra is on the menu, they know I'll order it—and macaroni and cheese!

James could save a penny till the head fell off. He used to tell me that he had buried a lot of money in the backyard and that I should dig it up after he died. I never saw any evidence that he had buried anything over the years, so I don't think that was true. But I did find cash he had saved in pockets and envelopes all throughout the house after he was gone. He was such a saver because he remembered the stories his parents told him about going through the Great Depression. He always wanted to be sure he had resources to do whatever needed to be done. James told me, "If you make life worth living, I'll make the living."

He never wanted me to want for anything or to have to depend on anybody. He often recited a little poem to me:

"Because your generous heart gives out a kindly thought a minute, you make the whole world better just by being in it."

James had a real sense of humor. He always wanted to save money and told me I would need money to live on after he was gone. He used to tell me that when he died, to not let the funeral home people talk me into purchasing an expensive casket to lay him to rest. He said he didn't

need that. Instead, he told me to ask them how much the casket cost. He said, "If they tell you they don't have anything less expensive, ask them, 'What did the casket come in?' They will probably tell you it came in a box. You then tell them you want the box." That's my favorite story about James. I even had his niece tell that one at his funeral.

These verses were read at James's funeral:

Anyone who listens to the word but does not do what it says is like a man who looks at his face in a mirror and, after looking at himself, goes away and immediately forgets what he looks like. But the man who looks intently into the perfect law that gives freedom, and continues to do this, not forgetting what he has heard, but doing it—he will be blessed in what he does. (James 1:23–25 NIV)

SELFIE 10

MY SUNDAY BEST: I had just purchased a royal blue maxi dress, so when I saw this hat, I knew I could pair it with that dress. Since then, I've also purchased this skirt and blouse set in the same color!

Family

In every conceivable manner, the family is
a link to our past, bridge to our future.

—ALEX HALEY

Although I didn't know my grandfathers, I knew my grandmothers. My father's mother, Elizabeth Ford, lived in Crockett, Texas. She wrote me a letter every month. It was the same thing: *How are you? I hope you are doing fine. I am fine.* But that was all right. Sometimes there would be a dollar in the envelope.

We took the train about once a year to visit Grandma Ford. We had "church on the grounds," where everybody gathered for an outdoor worship service followed by a delicious potluck feast of fried chicken, turkey, ham, collard greens, fresh corn, and more.

Those were the best times.

My maternal grandmother, Martha Howell, lived closer to us in

You're never too old to set another

goal or to dream a new dream.

-LES BROWN

Muskogee, Oklahoma, so we saw her all the time. She loved to bake cakes and let me lick the bowl of batter. I loved that.

Now that my parents, grandmothers, and beloved husband have passed away, my immediate family consists of my sister, Jewell, and her husband, Marvin, and their children, Marva La Verne (I'm honored she has my name) and Stephen. I have been blessed to see my niece and nephew grow up, marry, and have successful lives. I pray for them and their families daily. During the pandemic we started to have family Zoom calls every Sunday at 5:00 p.m. We are a close-knit group.

My dream is to have a place like the Kennedy compound in Hyannis Port, Massachusetts, where we all could live together. Strong, healthy families have love, compassion, forgiveness, trust, honesty, and respect in common. I am so grateful that my family has that in abundance.

Lord, thank You for family, those whose bloodlines I share and those who are my brothers and sisters in Christ. Bless and keep them always. Amen.

MY SUNDAY BEST: I'm very good at color and design, and I love coordinating my outfits. As you can see, the swirls in the hat match the swirls in my blazer. Yellow is like sunshine. It just brightens your day.

Freedom

I must admit that I have taken for granted the freedom I have to move about and worship as I please. I am a citizen of the United States and have lived here all my life. Freedom is something I've always had, and for eight decades and counting, I haven't had to live any other way.

I love being independent! I value my freedom and flexibility. I was on my own after college and lived as a single woman in Chicago until I married James Wimberly. But after making a commitment to be his wife, I had to consider him and his wishes when I made decisions. I didn't go and come as I pleased. James was very protective of me and always concerned about my safety. To keep the peace between us, I chose not to do some things or go certain places. I had a good marriage for forty-four years, but I chose to never remarry. Now, I can once again do whatever I want, whenever I want. I'm free as a bird.

But with freedom, there is responsibility. God gives us the freedom to choose every day. It's called free will. The Lord does not force us to love Him or to do what's right. We have a choice, but I always ask for His guidance because I want to do His will, not mine.

I will walk about in freedom,
for I have sought out your precepts.

(PSALM 119:45 NIV)

50

MY SUNDAY BEST: I bought this red hat to match my one-and-only red suit. It's a great hat, but it's a little plain, so I dressed it up with a pearl and rhinestone hat pin.

Mother

Resilience

In life, you have to learn how to bounce back.

Or at least stand firm through difficulties. I've faced all types of trials and disappointments, but by the grace of God I made it through them and kept moving.

One of my biggest challenges was when my parents died—twenty-six days apart. Daddy had been sick for decades after suffering a stroke when I was just seven years old. We lovingly took care of him all those years. He passed away on November 28, 1979, at the age of eighty-three. My dear mother, who had been diagnosed that spring with ALS, commonly known as Lou Gehrig's disease, soon followed and

went home to be with the Lord on Christmas Eve at age seventy-three. That was a devastating time for me. But I had to work and keep going. Although I had my moments of sorrow, I didn't have time for self-pity. I had to keep pushing forward.

Mother was my biggest inspiration when it comes to resilience. In my eyes, she could do anything. Although she battled a disease that slowly attacked her muscles to the point that she couldn't even flick a fly off her face, Mother soldiered on and made her family and God priorities throughout her life. She cooked and cleaned, taught Sunday school, and guided and counseled her children and others. Because we didn't have a car, she walked everywhere. The woman put in some miles every week. I never heard Mother complain about anything. Never. Talk about taking the lemons of life and making lemonade—that was my mother. It's from her that I got my ability to take any situation, one that would perhaps discourage or depress someone else, and push through it. That's why I couldn't let even a pandemic get me down. With God's grace, you've got to keep it moving.

Dear Lord, show me how to bounce back from whatever trials come my way. I need Your strength to keep on pushing and moving forward. In Jesus' name. Amen.

Dad

KEEP UP,

and you will

not have to

CATCH UP.

SELFIE 13

JUNE 21, 2020

MY SUNDAY BEST: On a trip to Italy, I bought this beautiful necklace, and when I got home, I purchased this beige suit to wear with it. The crystal earrings look great with both. Blessedly, I already had the hat that matched the ensemble.

My Top 20 Favorite Scriptures

Deuteronomy 31:8

Judges 6:14 and 16

Esther 4:14

Psalm 23:1–6

Psalm 34:19

Psalm 37:1

Isaiah 40:8

Isaiah 41:10

Habakkuk 2:2–4

Matthew 5:8

John 3:16

John 15:5

Galatians 6:9

Ephesians 3:20

Philippians 4:6–8

James 4:10

1 Peter 5:6–7

2 Peter 1:5–10

1 John 1:7–10

3 John 1:2

SELFIE 14

JUNE 28, 2020

MY SUNDAY BEST: I bought this white suit with gold trim to match a hat in my collection that was white and also trimmed with gold. I love the way my glasses, which are edged in rhinestones, add a little extra sparkle to this outfit.

Faith

We ought always to thank God for you, brothers
and sisters, and rightly so, because your faith
is growing more and more, and the love all
of you have for one another is increasing.

—2 THESSALONIANS 1:3 NIV

My faith has certainly grown over the years. It was faith that got me through my parents' back-to-back deaths when I was forty years old. Losing both in less than a month was not easy. It took something as devastating as that to get me to really dig deep into the Word, especially after I got over my initial sorrow. Although I had been in the church all my life, I didn't really have a close relationship with the Lord. Going to church all those years was just something that I did. But after Mother and Daddy died, that's when I got closer to the Lord and established a real relationship with Him. I realized that I had been going through the motions until then. I knew of God, but I didn't really *know* God. My faith in Jesus really began to take off after my parents left this earth.

I've found that the key to increasing my faith has been meditating on God's Word. The more I meditate on the Word, the less I focus on my fears. By simply reading the Bible and taking in what God says I've learned more about His character, His ways, and His promises. I get to encounter His presence and hear His voice.

After the death of my mother, I felt the need to draw closer to the Lord. So, I delved into the Word in an unconventional way. I typed out every word that Jesus ever said—all the red print in the King James Version. Every morning, for about a year and a half, I sat at my computer to type the Lord's words from Matthew, Mark, Luke, and John. I later decided to have all those sheets of paper bound as leather books, one for each Gospel. I consider that my greatest work in life—more than anything I've accomplished in my career.

I dedicated the finished books to my parents and my late husband, James. After I'm gone, I want them to go to my great-nephews Anthony and Adrian. I want them to start really reading the Bible and establish a relationship with the Lord.

During my morning devotions, I also read and reflect on the words of Jesus in different Bible translations beyond the King James Version. I diligently work my way through each of my bound Scripture books and then start over again. I also accompany that with readings from other devotional books.

More than a decade ago, I started typing out my favorite scriptures. I now have more than two hundred of them. They range from Psalm 46:1: "God is our refuge and strength, a very present help in trouble" to Matthew 6:33: "But seek ye first the kingdom of God, and his righteousness; and all these things shall be added unto you" (KJV). Many of those verses appear in this book.

I typed out the words of Jesus and my favorite scriptures to extend my relationship with the Lord. I wanted to make sure I knew what He would have me do. I want to live as righteously as I can, and I can't do that if I don't know what He says.

Thank You, Lord, that Your Word is a lamp
unto my feet and a light unto my path.

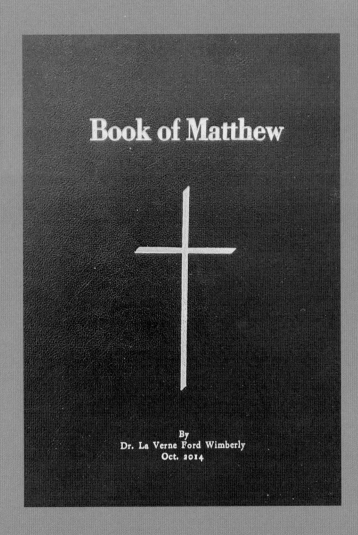

Book of Matthew

By
Dr. La Verne Ford Wimberly
Oct. 2014

SELFIE 15

JULY 5, 2020

MY SUNDAY BEST: My husband, James, used to call this my Robin Hood hat. It was made by the same milliner who made my favorite black hat. Now I have two hats by Fleur de Paris in New Orleans.

Beauty

I have seen such beautiful things created by God! The turquoise waters in Santorini, Greece, and Lake Louise in Canada's Banff National Park. The stunning Butchart Gardens in Victoria, British Columbia, and the awesome Great Wall of China as well as the majestic Grand Canyon in Arizona. Traveling the world has given me the opportunity to feast my eyes on God's handiwork in creation. I don't know how anyone can say there is no God when such unspeakable beauty and grandeur is on display throughout the world. I am in awe of it all.

I have never considered myself beautiful. I am tall—by the time

I was fifteen, I was five feet, ten and three-fourths inches—and I hated being that height when I was younger. It was especially hard being a tall girl. I was always in the back row for photos, and I didn't like being taller than the boys around me. That was *not* fun. I admit that I'm fine with my height now. I had looked forward to that great day when I would shrink as I aged. It's come! I am now five feet nine inches, and I'm okay with that.

While I've struggled with seeing my own beauty, I have always believed that true beauty comes from within. It can be seen in one's countenance. A smile can exude acceptance and love, the keys to building meaningful relationships

There is also beauty in knowing God. Knowing Him gives us the peace that we all seek. He only asks us to do as stated in the latter part of John 3:16: "For God so loved the world that he gave his one and only Son, that whoever believes in him shall not perish but have eternal life" (NIV). All the Lord asks of us is to believe in Jesus. It's that simple—and beautiful.

Dear Lord, thank You for the beautiful things and people that surround me every day. **Open my eyes** to Your beauty and most of all the beauty of knowing and loving You. In Jesus' name I pray. Amen.

SELFIE 16

MY SUNDAY BEST: This is just a plain tan hat, so I dressed it up with a colorful scarf!

Wimberly's Words of Wisdom

PREPARATION
is the key
to success.

PLAN YOUR
WORK and WORK
YOUR PLAN.

SELFIE 17

JULY 19, 2020

MY SUNDAY BEST: One of my art teachers at Dunbar Elementary used to chastise me for mixing primary and secondary colors together. I loved purple and fuchsia then, and I still love that combination now. My teacher said that the two colors didn't go together. I was ahead of my time!

Grace

One of my high school teachers, Mr. Booker T. Moore, was a grace-giver. If I didn't do well on a test or received a C or D on an assignment, I would throw myself on the mercy of Mr. Moore's court and ask for a do-over. He knew I had the where-withal to perform better. "Okay, Ford," he would say, and give me a new deadline. I didn't do that often, only a time or two. But every time I would do better. I thank God for Mr. Moore's grace.

Our teachers did all they could to support us and other students so that we would be successful. Mr. Moore was an example who inspired me to extend grace many times to my own students during the years I was in the classroom.

Lord, help me to extend the grace that You so graciously give to me. Amen.

The Lord
grants us grace
every day.
Grace is the gift that
keeps on giving.

SUNDAY BEST: I bought this hat on a cruise ship years ago. The
t my eye, and I loved the way it adorned the crown of the hat!

Friendship

No friendship is an accident.

—O. HENRY

Proverbs 18:24 says, "A man who has friends must himself be friendly" (NKJV). Mother used to say, "In order to have a friend, you have to be a friend."

I believe that.

My first friend, Marilyn Britton Mayes, lived two doors down from me. We've been friends since the early 1950s. We did everything together. Talk about somebody who could beg. Marilyn would beg my mother to let me go with her family to various places. *"Please, Mrs. Ford, let La Verne go and if you let her go this time, I won't ask you anymore."* And of course, Marilyn would be back to beg

the very next day. Marilyn and I may not talk to each other every month, but when we do, it's a marathon.

Marilyn's dad was a teacher, and she became one too. In fact, she was the one who invited me to come to Chicago to seek a teaching position when I couldn't find a job in Tulsa after college. That invitation and my decision to go changed my life.

I've had some wonderful friends throughout my career. Bobbie Allen Booker is one of the most loyal people I know. Bobbie succeeded me as principal at George Washington Carver Middle School. You can't say anything bad about me around

A sweet friendship
refreshes the soul.

—Proverbs 27:9 MSG

Bobbie Booker. That is not going to happen. She will stop you and stand up for me. And I do the same for her.

Loyalty is essential in a friendship. Friends like Bobbie are loyal. They will not undermine you. There were times when positions at work became available and I wouldn't apply for them because I knew a friend was interested. Sometimes you step back or step aside so that a friend can get ahead. Your time will come, and that person will be there for you. It's called supporting each other.

While I have been surrounded by faithful and loving friends, my greatest friend has been Jesus. He's one I can share everything with—my hopes and fears, my faults and failures. And He will still love me. John 15:13 NIV tells us, "Greater love has no one than this: to lay down one's life for one's friends." That's what Jesus did for me. He's that kind of friend.

School Days
1951–55

School Days
1952–53

Dear Lord, let me be the loving and faithful friend You have commanded me to be, just as You have been to me. In Jesus' name. Amen.

74

SELFIE 19

AUGUST 2, 2020

MY SUNDAY BEST: By now you know that I love black-and-white hats, and here's another! I'm wearing a suite of jewelry that includes earrings, necklace, and a brooch, but I thought the hat was a little plain, so I put the brooch on my hat.

A Few of My Favorite Things

Attending church

Traveling, especially cruising (I have been to all fifty states and several foreign countries)

Clothes shopping

Playing and working various kinds of games and puzzles

Reading psychology journals

Eating out at famous restaurants

Dancing

Spinning (cycling)

Walking around the track at my health club

Participating in competitive activities (*Tulsa Run, Williams Route 66 Half Marathon*)

Socializing with family and friends

Volunteering, being of service to those in need

Listening to music (Gospel, rhythm and blues, soul, jazz, classical, reggae, opera, etc.)

Home decorating

Watching TV

Taking pictures

Enjoying life

SELFIE 20

AUGUST 9, 2020

MY SUNDAY BEST: Every once in a while I think it's fun to change from the more formal to the informal, which is why I chose to wear this fun pink sun hat with a vibrant scarf as an accent.

Do unto others
as you would have
others do unto you.

SELFIE 21

AUGUST 16, 2020

MY SUNDAY BEST: I bought this hat from an African American lady who was selling hats out of her home. Since one can never have too many black and white hats, I added this one to my collection! The black-and-white applique around the neckline of my sweater is a lovely counterpoint to the hat, black-and-white pendant, and earrings.

Kindness

I once read somewhere,

"Be kind to everyone you meet because everyone is fighting a battle."

Those words have stuck with me. You may not see it or know it, but deep down someone has something going on in their life and they could benefit from your random, or deliberate act of kindness.

I've always tried to be kind to everyone. It harkens back to the Golden Rule I constantly heard as a child: "Do unto others as you would have others do unto you." We heard that everywhere—in school, at church, in the beauty shop, at home. Unfortunately, so many people today are looking out for themselves and their interests instead of looking out for others. That's so sad.

When I was growing up, people showed so many kindnesses to my family and me. Neighbors showered us with gifts at Christmastime because they knew our situation with my father's illness. They included us in their family outings and trips. Because of them we wanted for nothing.

I am grateful for the kindness and respect I was shown in my position as a Black woman educator and administrator. I am constantly amazed at how people I don't know, but who know me, still pay me respect and honor.

I remain awed by the outpouring of kindness I've received from people all over the country who were touched or inspired by my "Zoom church" story after it went viral. I still can't believe I received so many wonderful presents! People made quite an effort, too, sending the gifts to my church in hopes that they would get to me. Earlier in the book you saw photos of some of the items: gorgeous hats; (some with matching outfits); a one-of-its-kind hand-painted jacket; beautiful jewelry; acrylic paintings; and ceramic tiles with images of me in my church hats. I have been overwhelmed by such kindness and generosity. I never expected any of that. Despite all the negative things you may hear about humanity today, people are still very kind.

The Lord has been so good to me too. His lovingkindness cannot be matched by anyone. Psalm 26:3 says, "For Your lovingkindness is before my eyes, and I have walked in Your truth" (NKJV). I see it, I recognize it, and I'm going to keep walking in it.

Lord, You have been so kind. May I always show kindness to everyone and point them to You. In Your name I pray. Amen.

SELFIE 22

AUGUST 23, 2020

MY SUNDAY BEST: Years ago, James and I went on a cruise, and I bought this nautical hat to match the nautical blouse that I'm wearing.

Encouragement

Life is too short to miss encouraging someone who may be going through a tough time. You never know when it's your turn to face difficulties and you may need someone to encourage you. Everyone should take onus to encourage someone. My family and friends say that I'm an encourager. I'm the one who will ask, "How can I help?" or say, "You can get through this" when I feel a person needs to know that someone cares about them.

There have been lots of people to cheer me on throughout my life. I grew up in an era when the saying "It takes a village" was really true. Church members, neighbors, teachers—we had a lot of help back in those days. Everyone wanted to see us do well and be successful. You couldn't get away with just being mediocre. You had to be on top of your game and be the best. And they helped you do that.

SELFIE 23

AUGUST 30, 2020

MY SUNDAY BEST: I bought this plain straw hat at a little market in Israel. I adore this lavender floral suit and think it makes the hat look much better.

Perseverance

Let perseverance finish its work so that you may
be mature and complete, not lacking anything.

—JAMES 1:4 NIV

I've found that as we age, we must persevere and never cease to learn. You can't give up on life when things don't go your way. With the help of the Lord, you can make it.

Desperate times will push you to persevere so that you can survive. In 2009, after a blizzard in Tulsa that kept folks in their homes for days, I taught myself how to use social media to beat isolation and boredom. I had kept hearing about Facebook, so I went online to learn more about it. I became a social media junkie! It broadened my world and helped me to stay connected to people. That wouldn't have happened if I hadn't persevered through the learning curve.

Also, some of the decisions that were made by others that affected my career could have pushed me to give up, but instead I persevered. Take for example the time I was demoted by the superintendent of Tulsa schools.

I was middle school director at the time. A new superintendent came in and decided to reorganize. He moved me into the role of director of alternative education, which was a lower position than what I held. While I was disappointed and sad, I didn't quit. I kept going and showed up to do the job. I had to do a lot of praying during that time. I always kept my electronic Bible on my desk and turned to it whenever I needed guidance or to calm myself when something happened to upset my spirit. A few years later, there was another superintendent change. As a result, a new administrator was brought in as my supervisor. Each morning I read Scripture to prepare myself to face a boss who didn't have any compassion or respect for me.

I kept the faith knowing that God would elevate me in His own time. I knew in my heart that the Lord would eventually place me in a position that I really wanted. And He did. In the end, despite the setback, I was able to continue to move up the ladder to become interim superintendent of Tulsa schools. That was in 2000, and I was the first African American to hold that position. Only God could do such a thing!

And He's done so many other things for me too! Here are some other "firsts" God's allowed me to enjoy over the years:

Photo credit Turner Goodrum

— First Black . . .

First Black to work in the City
of Tulsa customer service
department (1964)

— First Black Female . . .

First Black female principal of a Tulsa
Public School junior high school (1982)

First Black female assistant superintendent for curriculum and instruction
in Tulsa Public Schools (1995–2000)

First Black female deputy superintendent Tulsa Public Schools
(2000–2004)

First Black female to become a superintendent in Tulsa Public Schools
(March–August 2000). In recognition of my TPS interim
superintendent tenure, the mayor declared September 16, 2000,
La Verne Ford Wimberly Day!

First Black female to have a media center (library) named for an individual
in a Tulsa Public Schools high school (2004)

— First Inaugural Class . . .

First inaugural class of the Oklahoma African American Educators Hall
of Fame, Inc. (September 2011)

SELFIE 24

SEPTEMBER 6, 2020

MY SUNDAY BEST: I don't go to horse races anymore, but this hat reminds me of when I did. This hat is so unique, it has a white rose on top, and one beneath the brim. Isn't it interesting?

> A gentle answer turns away wrath,
> but a harsh word stirs up anger.
> The tongue of the wise adorns knowledge.
>
> —PROVERBS 15:1–2 NIV

Gentleness

I was reared hearing the wise statement, "You can catch more flies with honey than with vinegar."

That expression really came in handy, around 1969 to 1971 at the height of desegregation. I was pulled out of the classroom and appointed as an adjustment counselor. In that role, I was among those who helped desegregate the Tulsa Public School system. I was assigned to Cleveland Junior High and Hamilton Junior High. It was my job to defray racial conflict and to do that I had to be filled with compassion, show compassion, and treat all students as human, despite their behavior. I quickly learned that if a student displayed any racial antagonism, it had been learned in the home. But acting with compassion influenced the behavior at school.

A student at Hamilton Junior High said, "I realize that you can't do everything, but it helps me to know that we have someone who listens and cares about us."

As a school administrator, I faced some highly volatile situations. I encountered hostile parents and staff related to decisions to suspend or expel students. To avoid negative repercussions, I learned to listen intently with empathy to hear the person out before stating the policy or my position. I am convinced that my wise decision years ago to remain silent until a man had his say kept me from physical harm.

He was extremely irate because his son had been suspended and that I, a Black woman, had the authority and audacity to make the recommendation. He was very tall and intimidating, pacing back and forth with his fist raised as he yelled profanities at me. The unnerving part about his tirade was that I was alone in the office at the time. I remained quiet for thirty minutes while he ranted and raved, and then, with my voice laced with honey, the LORD gave me a few sentences to say that changed the man's perspective. He accepted his son's punishment and left the office.

I know God protected me in that situation, and He gave me wisdom and guidance on how to handle it. Sometimes the best—and wisest—option is silence, followed by a few choice words from the LORD.

MY SUNDAY BEST: Fuchsia is one of my favorite colors. A friend was getting married, and the guests were asked to wear hats to the bridal shower, so I bought this hat for that occasion. Later, I purchased this beautiful blouse with multicolored rhinestones cascading down the sleeves.

Wimberly's Words of Wisdom

You can
overcome
FAILURE
with a
CAN-DO
attitude.

MY SUNDAY BEST: I purchased this hat at a trunk show. The gold-and-black chain caught my eye, and it had a matching purse, so I got both! A classic black hat is always a good accessory to have on hand. You can never have too many. Black is always in style!

Fear

So do not fear, for I am with you;
do not be dismayed, for I am your God.
I will strengthen you and help you;
I will uphold you with my righteous right hand.

—ISAIAH 41:10 NIV

I have a real fear of dogs, cats, and public speaking. These are the things that cause me the most trauma. I know the Word says that God did not give us a spirit of fear, but there are still some things that unsettle and frighten me.

When I was much younger, I was afraid that I wouldn't get to attend college or have a successful career. I didn't think I was smart enough or had what it takes. I also feared being alone at home because I thought someone would break in and attack me. As a child, I was so fearful, I never wanted to take a bath if my family was not near the bathroom. It was particularly frightening at night during the summer months when my family was outside on the porch, and I had to take a bath before bedtime. I would be in and out of that tub in less than sixty seconds!

I'm also a germaphobe. I think

my fear of germs and obsession with cleanliness was a good thing during the pandemic. I was way ahead of the directives from the Centers for Disease Control and Prevention to constantly wash your hands and wipe down countertops. I had already been doing that. I didn't even bring the newspaper inside my home after it was delivered. The fear of COVID-19 kept me healthy during that time.

Despite my fears, I have forged ahead. Whenever I had to make presentations for my job—or even speak now at various events—I somehow manage to temporarily overcome my anxiety about speaking in front of others. I know the Lord gives me the strength to stand up tall, face the people, open my mouth, and let the words come out. It certainly isn't my doing!

"For God hath not given us the spirit of fear; but of power, and of love, and of a sound mind." (2 Timothy 1:7 KJV)

Father God, thank You for the fears You have helped me to overcome—and for those You will help me to conquer. In Jesus' name. Amen

Wimberly's
Words of Wisdom

KNOWLEDGE

is

POWER.

MY SUNDAY BEST: One of my best friends, Loretta Collier, gave me this hat just before she died. Loretta had glaucoma and was losing her eyesight, but she could see well enough to purchase this beautiful hat for me as a thank you for helping her around on our trip to Italy.

Top 10 Life Lessons

1

Success begins when you take the first step.

2

You cannot succeed without making an effort.

3

To finish, you must start.

4

A good reputation is better than material wealth.

5

How you respond to life's challenges
is within your control.

6

Life is what you make it.

7

Your future, your choice.

8

Your thoughts mirror your destiny.

9

Your greatest asset is your health.

10

Everything must change, nothing remains the same.

SELFIE 28

OCTOBER 4, 2020

MY SUNDAY BEST: Bling, bling, bling, and more bling! About seven months into the pandemic when our church held its first outdoor service, I put on a mask *and* a shield. True to my fashion, everything I wore was covered in bling! It was great to see so many of my fellow congregants in person, and I got lots of compliments on my outfit.

The Lord's Prayer

Our Father which art in heaven,
　　Hallowed be thy name.
Thy kingdom come, Thy will be done in
　　earth, as it is in heaven.
Give us this day our daily bread.
And forgive us our debts, as we forgive
　　our debtors.
And lead us not into temptation, but
　　deliver us from evil: For thine is the
　　kingdom, and the power, and the
　　glory, for ever. Amen.

(MATTHEW 6:9–13 KJV)

Pray

Therefore I tell you, whatever you ask
for in prayer, believe that you have
received it, and it will be yours.

—MARK 11:24 NIV

My first encounter with prayer was the Lord's Prayer, which I learned as a child. Through prayer I also learned that God is my all in all. I talk to Him quietly throughout the day, every day.

His Word says ask and it shall be given. I have no problem asking God to provide a parking space for me on a busy street or clearing the traffic so that I can make it to an appointment on time. Some might say those are frivolous prayers, but I ask the Lord for what I need whenever I need it. He answers those prayers.

God certainly can answer prayers in unconventional ways. Years ago, my husband told me he needed a new car because the old one was racking up big repair bills. I told him not to worry; I was going to win him a new car. He didn't seem to quite believe me, but I prayed about it.

In the meantime, our local newspaper and a convenience store chain were sponsoring a contest.

The grand prize: a brand-new Chevy Trailblazer. I decided to fill out the entry form in James's name. A drawing was held to choose several finalists from all the entries—and my husband was one of them! I kept praying and telling James that he was going to win. The finalists gathered one day and each picked a key from a container and tried to start the car. Lo and behold, my husband chose the winning key! We kept that car for thirteen years before I gave it to my great-nephews. You can't tell me what God won't do when you keep praying and believing.

Thank You, Lord, for hearing my prayers and answering them in Your own way. Amen.

SELFIE 29

OCTOBER 11, 2020

MY SUNDAY BEST: I don't stop wearing white the day after Labor Day, I love to wear it all year! I'm wearing a simple wool hat in winter white. I took this selfie leading up to the November election. I wore my necklace to remind everyone to vote.

FAILURE

is not an

OPTION.

SELFIE 30

OCTOBER 18, 2020

MY SUNDAY BEST: I like this outfit because of the militaristic look: black trim with white applique. The crown of the hat is trimmed in gold braid.

My Gospel Playlist

"There Is a Praise Ringing in My Soul"

"He Knows How Much We Can Bear"

"Through It All"

"The Lord's Prayer"

"Pass Me Not O, Gentle Savior"

"This Place"

"Total Praise"

"Changed"

"Encourage Yourself"

"They Got the Word"

"God Favored Me"

"Lord Help Me to Hold Out"

"I Need Thee Every Hour"

"Old Rugged Cross"

"Jerusalem"

"Now Behold the Lamb"

"Safe in His Arms"

"The Lord Keeps on Blessing Me"

"He's My Everything"

"Something Happens"

"Center of My Joy"

"Emmanuel"

"We Offer Praise"

"He Promised Me"

"God's Grace"

"I'm on My Way to Heaven"

MY SUNDAY BEST: Years ago, at Central High School, I worked with Bernice Velie, a home economics teacher. She purchased this hat for herself but decided it was too flamboyant for her, so she gave it to me! I cherish this hat and Bernice's kindness.

Be Bold!

The righteous are as bold as a lion.

—PROVERBS 28:1 NIV

Sometimes you must have the courage to go against the grain and not fear what others think of you. You have to be bold and stand up for what is right, regardless of what people may say or the repercussions that come from your actions.

In 1958 I was a sophomore at the University of Tulsa. There were only about ten Black students on campus. I had a very prejudiced professor for a class in psychology, which was my major. At that time, grades for tests and assignments were posted outside the classroom door for everyone to see. One of my classmates, a young White woman named Melinda, noticed that I always got Ds and Fs. She came to me one day and said my grades puzzled her because I participated in class and knew the material. Melinda said she thought that some racial prejudice was going on. So she came up with a plan to see if that was true.

Melinda suggested that the next time we had an exam, we would complete it and then trade papers. I would put my name on her exam, and she would put her name on mine. Sure enough, the paper with my name on it, which was really hers, received a D; the test with her name on it (which was my exam) received an A. We continued to do this for a while. Melinda and I finally took the graded papers to the dean of the college and explained the situation. We both were doing good work, but I was the one getting the poor grades. The dean said he'd look into it. However, he discouraged me from filing a complaint. He didn't want any public fallout to stop me from getting my degree. In the end, the dean changed my final grade.

I still praise God that I was able to withstand the doings of a racist professor and graduate with my degree. I often think about Melinda and wonder what happened to her. It was a bold move on her part to stand up for me, and I will never forget her.

Isaiah 54:17 says, "No weapon formed against you shall prosper" (NKJV). I know this for sure. The Lord has shown me that more than once.

Being bold isn't always easy. But with God on your side, you will be all right.

Dear Lord, please give me a bold spirit to stand up for what is good and right in Your sight. Amen.

Forgiveness

Be kind and compassionate to one
another, forgiving each other, just
as in Christ God forgave you.

—EPHESIANS 4:32 NIV

Nobody is perfect—and Lord knows I'm not. We make mistakes, say and do things we shouldn't, and step out of God's will to satisfy our own selfish desires. That's when we often ask for forgiveness from God and from one another.

I learned a wonderful lesson in forgiveness from my sister. In 1961, Jewell had been teaching in Missouri and decided to move back to Tulsa. She bought her first car: a spanking brand-new, bronze Chevy. It was beautiful. She even let me drive it.

One day I borrowed the Chevy to go to the laundromat and all was well . . . until my return home. I had put the freshly cleaned and folded laundry in a basket on the back seat. As I made a turn on to another street, I noticed the basket was sliding off the seat. So, what did I do? I turned my head to push the basket back onto the seat to keep it from falling on the floor. Before I knew it, I had crashed into a telephone pole! The car was badly damaged, and I was mortified.

I will never forget Jewell's reaction. "Accidents happen," was all she said. Jewell wasn't angry. She didn't berate me or make me feel guilty about wrecking her beautiful new car. She was gracious. And I was ever so grateful. Everyone needs forgiveness at some point in their life. I certainly needed it then.

Father God, please give me a forgiving spirit when others offend or persecute me. Help me to remember that You forgive me repeatedly, day after day, and I should be quick to do the same—just as Jewell did when I wrecked her car! In Jesus' name. Amen.

SELFIE 32

NOVEMBER 1, 2020

MY SUNDAY BEST: I bought this hat from a Black merchant in New Orleans. The ornaments on the hat are gold-plated. How's that for bling?

The best

PREPARATION

for the future IS DOING

YOUR BEST

TODAY.

Grit

Let thine eyes look right on, and let thine
eyelids look straight before thee.

—PROVERBS 4:25 KJV

When you have to hang in there to get it done, that's true grit, as they say. You may face struggles and all kinds of battles to accomplish your goals, but you keep pushing, you keep going until the very end.

I first heard about Mary McLeod Bethune when I was in the fourth grade. She became my first shero. Dr. Bethune was an educator, philanthropist, and civil rights activist. She also founded Bethune-Cookman University in Daytona Beach, Florida, in 1904 with just $1.50. The school still exists today as one of the nation's Historically Black Colleges and Universities. I admire her for opening a college in the face of all manner of opposition. That took stick-to-itiveness. And in my mind, Mary McLeod Bethune gets extra bonus points because she was tall, just like me. I could relate to her!

Dear Lord, thank You for the examples You have given me of those who stuck close to You to reach the goals You had set for them. Please grant me the grit I need to do the same. Amen.

Reading from Dr. Mary McLeod Bethune's autobiography to a group of students.

Dr. Bethune in her office in Washington, DC.

SELFIE 33

NOVEMBER 8, 2020

MY SUNDAY BEST: I call this outfit my "Petals of Praise," because of the rhinestones that adorn the petals. I love the way the hat and blouse go with the pearl and rhinestone necklace and earrings!

Joy

May the God of hope fill you with all joy and peace
as you trust in him, so that you may overflow
with hope by the power of the Holy Spirit.

—ROMANS 15:13 NIV

When you can wake up in the morning, that's joy! Many people take opening their eyes each day for granted. Not me. I always think, *This is the day that the Lord has made; let us rejoice and be glad in it* (Psalm 118:24 ESV). When you can wake up, put your feet on the floor, and get up, that's a blessing. I don't understand people who go around filled with anger all the time. You've got to have something good going on in your life!

What a joy it is to move. I go to a spin class three times a week. I'm the oldest one among the cyclists and I'm happy to say that I can keep up with the best of them. I love the loud music. I also walk and lift weights several times a week. Being able to move about brings me great joy. Scripture says it is in Him that we live and move and have our being. I certainly believe that.

Trust in the LORD and do good;

dwell in the land and enjoy safe pasture.

—PSALM 37:3 NIV

There are so many things that God has created for us to enjoy. I appreciate all He has given me to live life to the fullest. I like to explore places I have only read about. I have been privileged to see the indescribable beauty of countries like Greece, Scotland, China, Bermuda, Mexico, Ghana, and other nations in the Caribbean. I've also had the pleasure of traveling to all fifty states and experiencing what each has to offer. And I enjoy and appreciate the simple pleasures of gathering with family for holiday dinners, meeting up with old friends to reconnect, and spending quiet time at a local park to bask in nature. Helping others also brings me great enjoyment and satisfaction.

People say laughter is the best medicine. I truly enjoy laughing at good, clean jokes and seeing people do silly things where nobody gets hurt. Late night talk show host Trevor Noah cracks me up too. I love his humor and insights on current events.

As I grow older, I find myself thinking about the past more often and enjoying some great childhood memories. One of my favorites is Thanksgiving Day when we had the big high school football game between Muskogee's Manual Training and Tulsa's Booker T. Washington. Wherever the game was played, my family like many others got together for the fun. I loved hearing wild stories about past players, victories, and losses. Everybody came dressed to the nines for the event. I'm talking about men decked out in suits and ties, and women strutting in dresses, heels, and stylish hats. Yes, for a football game!

I believe that the Lord wants His children to have a good life and enjoy the riches He provides for us here on earth. We don't have to wait to get to heaven to take pleasure in all that He has for us.

Here are my exercise tips:

Consult your doctor before you start your fitness regime.

Select exercises you enjoy.

Build exercise into your weekly schedule.

Determine what time of day works best for you (morning, midday, or evening).

Set a goal each week.

Be consistent.

Strive to get in a minimum of 150 minutes of exercise each week. (Try to do 30 minutes a day, five times per week!)

Challenge yourself.

Exercise with a friend or family member. Accountability helps.

Include cardio, strength training, and flexibility activities into your weekly routine.

If you're new to exercise, start at your own pace and don't focus on what others are doing.

Take a class or buy a fitness device.

Make it fun.

Listen to your favorite playlist while you exercise.

Celebrate your accomplishments!

Father God, You are the giver of good things. I am so grateful for Your love and generosity. I take great pleasure in Your gifts. Thank You for each one of them. In Jesus' name. Amen.

SELFIE 34

NOVEMBER 15, 2020

MY SUNDAY BEST: Brown wool hat accented with satin, velvet, and rhinestones. I purchased it from an African American lady who once owned a store here in Tulsa.

> In everything I did, I showed you that by this kind of hard work we must help the weak, remembering the words the Lord Jesus himself said: "It is more blessed to give than to receive."
>
> —ACTS 20:35 NIV

Serve

I have a real need to serve others, especially people in trouble. That urgent desire began in high school. I was a member of the Courtesy and Service Club, which rendered service to the school and promoted a feeling of good fellowship between students and the staff. I participated in Future Teachers of America, which inspired students to cultivate the qualities of successful teaching—and I didn't even have plans at that time to become an educator. Teachers certainly serve others. I also was a member of the

Junior Red Cross. I simply loved helping those in need.

The motivation to continue serving others after high school came while reading Luke 12:48: "From everyone who has been given much, much will be demanded; and from the one who has been entrusted with much, much more will be asked." I knew I had to do what the Lord expected of me because He had blessed me with so much.

I have spent most of my adult life serving others in various ways. I've helped feed the homeless, visited the sick and shut-ins, connected people with much-needed social services, and periodically provided financial assistance. As a result, I have received a considerable number of awards for my dedication to community service. One of the most memorable and cherished was the 2002 "Keeping the Dream Alive" Award presented to me by Tulsa's Martin Luther King Jr. Commemoration Society. For years, I spent countless hours assisting with the organization's annual King celebration activities. To be given an award in the name of Dr. King was an absolute honor. One of his most famous quotes is, "Everybody can be great . . . because anybody can serve. You don't have to have a college degree to serve. You don't have to make your subject and verb agree to serve. You only need a heart full of grace. A soul generated by love." That is so true.

The Lord calls each of us to be our brother's and sister's keeper. Every person has the ability to do something to encourage or lift someone's spirits when life is difficult. Service is simply giving of yourself.

Dear Lord, show me how I can serve someone today. And may I do so joyfully and graciously. Amen.

"Life's most persistent and urgent question is, 'What are you doing for others?'"

—DR. MARTIN LUTHER KING JR.

Advice to My Younger Self

Be bold. Be brave.

Live your life to the fullest.

You will not always get what you want.

Life is replete with situations
that require give-and-take.

Life is filled with many ups and
downs but keep moving forward.

Embrace change.

Do not sweat the small stuff.

Measure yourself against yourself,
rather than against others.

You are your best motivator.

Start saving for your retirement
with your first job.

Spend a little, save a lot.

Establish a network of support.

Take full responsibility for an enriched life.

Don't be afraid to give.

SELFIE 35

MY SUNDAY BEST: I purchased this incredible turquoise hat from a lady here in Tulsa. This is my #1 winter favorite. Isn't it a showstopper?

Light

And God said, "Let there be light," and there was light.

—GENESIS 1:3

Oh, how I love light! It energizes me. The first thing I do in the morning is open the drapes in my home so that light can come in. I don't know how people can sit in darkness. That's so depressing. My husband, James, used to work late as a police officer, so he came home at night. He used to say our house looked like a landing field at the airport because I had so many lights on. What can I say? It's all true.

Light is so important to me that I even refer to it in my email signature: "Walk in the Light." It reminds me that my behavior should always model Jesus, the light of the world. And I want to remind people to do the same.

My parents first introduced me to Jesus, the true light. I heard them talk about Him and saw them reading His Word every day. I learned more about Jesus through Bible stories in Sunday school and why He should matter to me. I grew up singing "This Little Light of Mine"— *This little light of mine, I'm gonna let it shine. Let it shine, let it shine, let it shine!* That's such a happy song. I told you, light makes me happy.

People can be filled with light too. Those are the ones who enter a room and everyone is glad to see them because they exude so much joy, happiness, and peace. My high school classmate Patricia Beck was like that. She was a beautiful person with a beautiful personality. I admired her for her radiance.

There are so many references to light in the Bible. I really like Psalm 119 NIV where it says, "Your word is a lamp for my feet, a light on my path" (v. 105) and "The unfolding of your words gives light; it gives understanding to the simple" (v. 130). If you follow the light-filled path of Jesus throughout your life, you can't go wrong. His light motivates you to move forward.

Thank You, Jesus, for being light in this dark world.
May I also be a light to those around me.
In Your precious name I pray. Amen.

Purpose

*And we know that in all things God works for
the good of those who love him, who have
been called according to his purpose.*

—ROMANS 8:28 NIV

I believe my purpose is to serve. That's why I don't mind volunteering and serving on all the boards and committees I'm currently a member of. I started to realize my purpose when I heard the commencement address at my high school graduation in 1956. It was delivered by Dr. Samuel P. Massie, a renowned scientist who worked on the Manhattan Project and became the first Black professor at the U.S. Naval Academy. Dr. Massie took his speech from Esther 4:14: *"For if you remain silent at this time, relief and deliverance for the Jews will arise from another place, but you and your father's family will perish. And who knows but that you have come to your royal position for such a time as this?"*

Dr. Massie's message was that Queen Esther was able to courageously save her Jewish people despite all the odds against her. And we could do something great too—we just had to figure it out. That really spoke to me. It resonated in my spirit. Fast forward forty years later, I got to meet Dr. Massie at an educators' conference! I had the opportunity to tell him that I remembered that long-ago commencement address and told him verbatim what he had said. He was flabbergasted that his words would be remembered by a seventeen-year-old high school senior.

How could I forget?

Those words changed my life.

As a child I had plans to travel around the world to fulfill my own selfish desires, but the Lord had other plans for me. I know I was destined by God to be an educator. It was and is my purpose, along with serving Him.

THE STATE OF OKLAHOMA

Commendations

Honoring the Life of

Dr. LaVerne Ford Wimberly

"Tulsa's Hometown Hero"

Whereas, Dr. LaVerne Wimberly, an educator for over forty years, advancing from classroom teacher through adjustment and class counselor, dean of students to assistant principal in junior and high schools, interim principal of a high school, middle school principal to Director of Middle Level Education, Director of Counseling and Social Services, Alternative Programs/Gifted and Talented/Summer school, Assistant Superintendent for Curriculum and Instruction, Interim Superintendent, Deputy Superintendent for School Operations, and Assistant Superintendent for Public Schools of Choice and Family Ombudsman Services, has dedicated her life to the continuing academic achievements to help all people reach their goals, dedicating her life's work to providing quality learnings to every child without exception; and

Whereas, Dr. LaVerne Wimberly graduated from Booker T. Washington High School in 1956, continuing her education at the University of Tulsa, where she received her Bachelor's Degree in Clinical Psychology in 1961; a Master's Degree in Teacher Education in 1961; a Master of Teaching Arts in 1970; a Doctorate of Education in Administration from Nova Southeastern University in 1989; and attended the Graduate School of Education in 1995, Summer Institute, Harvard University; and

Whereas, Dr. LaVerne Wimberly made history when she became the first African American female assistant at the secondary level in 1975. Continuing on her path of upward mobility and shattering glass ceilings, Dr. Wimberly became the first African American female Interim Superintendent for Tulsa Public Schools in 2000; and

Whereas, insomuch as it is fitting and proper, the Oklahoma State Legislature, acting on behalf of the citizens of Oklahoma, recognizes and commends the life, work and legacy of Dr. LaVerne Wimberly and her indelible impact in the realm of K-12 public education and Christian Education.

Now, therefore, pursuant to the joint motion of

Senator Kevin L. Matthews

Representative Regina Goodwin • Representative Monroe Nichols

the Oklahoma State Legislature extends to

Dr. LaVerne Ford Wimberly

sincere congratulations and directs that this citation be presented.

Senator Kevin L. Matthews
Senate District 11

Representative Regina Goodwin
House District 73

Representative Monroe Nichols
House District 72

Write the vision and make it plain.
—Habakkuk 2:2 NKJV

Vision

I believe you're never too old to have a vision.

About ten years ago, I started creating vision boards. A vision board is a visual representation of your goals. At the start of each year, I sit down with a stack of magazines and clip out various words, headlines and pictures that inspire and remind me of what I'd like to accomplish during the year. I paste those words on construction paper and put it where I can see it. My 2020 vision board featured wording such as "Wander Woman," "Live Victoriously," "Don't Settle for Sparse," "Find Your Holy Grail," "Take a New Chance," "Keep Aspiring," "The Unprocessed Life," "Join the Feel-Good Movement!," and "The Savviest Way to Save."

Oh, I had plans and high hopes for 2020. Then *bam!*—the pandemic hit. My dreams of traveling, staying healthy, and trying new things took a hit too. I figured the pandemic was the Lord's work and He was in control. There was nothing I could do about it and I just had to go with the flow. God does not make mistakes. So my focus shifted to staying safe, staying connected with others by posting my Sunday selfies and in various other ways, and staying even closer to the Lord. Concentrating on those things helped get me through one of the most challenging years of my life.

Having a vision to focus on has served me well. As I like to say, focus until you get it done!

Dear Lord, please reveal Your plans for me and may I focus on Your will, not mine. Guide me as I take steps to fulfill those plans and help me to trust You every step of the way. In Jesus' name. Amen.

SELFIE 36

NOVEMBER 29, 2020

MY SUNDAY BEST: I purchased this suit in the fall of 2000 after I completed my tenure as interim superintendent of the Tulsa Public School System. The photo of me wearing this outfit still hangs in Tulsa's Education Service Center on a wall filled with photos of all the past superintendents.

In my life,
the Lord has calmed more
storms than I can count
and always brought me
back to a peaceful state.

Y BEST: A fellow teacher, Bernice Velie, gave me this na
e she thought it looked better on me than it did on her.
accent? Maybe she thought I'd like it because of the ba
equins—bling! This hat looks lovely with my blue and bl
d another blue hat and this one is trimmed with a bit c

Success requires

☑ **LEARNING,**

☑ **STUDYING,**

☑ **HARD WORK,**

☑ **PERSEVERANCE,**

☑ and **DEDICATION.**

SELFIE 38

DECEMBER 13, 2020

MY SUNDAY BEST: This is my second favorite winter hat! It's the same design as my turquoise hat (Selfie 35).

Onward

*I press on toward the goal to win the
prize for which God has called me
heavenward in Christ Jesus.*

—PHILIPPIANS 3:14 NIV

Don't ever let hindrances or
obstacles stand in your way.

Before the pandemic hit, I
pressed on when my travel plans fell
through for a cruise to the Bahamas.
My sister was all set to go with me
but then she couldn't. I didn't want
to miss the cruise. I'm always on
board for the maiden voyages of
brand-new Royal Caribbean ships,
and I refused to allow an unexpected
change in plans stop me. Instead of
letting disappointment overtake me,
I decided to pack my bags and travel
solo for the weeklong ocean cruise.
As the song says, "onward, Christian
soldier." I forged ahead all by myself
and had a wonderful time.

Sometimes we're faced with
circumstances where we must press
onward. Many years ago, I chipped a
bone in my knee after falling off my
ten-speed bicycle. I was on crutches
for two weeks. The worst part of all,
I was an assistant principal and had
to maneuver three flights of stairs
during the day. With junior high
schoolers engaged in questionable
activities, I had to keep moving to
stay on top of things. It was not easy,
but I did it with dignity and survived
with God's grace.

SELFIE 39

DECEMBER 20, 2020

MY SUNDAY BEST: I bought this hat to match my full-length red-and-black rabbit coat! Since then, I've had the coat shortened to three-quarter length to get more use out of it. Even in Tulsa I enjoy wearing my fur coat three or four times a season.

Witness

While I am a bold witness for the Lord today, I haven't always been that way. One of my biggest regrets is that while I was working in the school district, I was more focused on upholding school policies and procedures that prohibited using the name of Jesus in any form. We couldn't even have nativity scenes or mention Jesus so as not to offend people of other faiths. I wasn't as bold then as I am now. I truly regret not standing up to oppose those policies. It probably would have cost me my job. But I still wish I had spoken up for Jesus then.

I've had people who have been great witnesses of faith to me—my parents, church leaders, family members, and friends. That's why I like Hebrews 12:1: "Therefore, since we are surrounded by such a great cloud of witnesses, let us throw off everything that hinders and the sin that so easily entangles." I pray that I can be that type of witness for someone along the way.

Dear Lord, please give me the courage to be a bold witness for You. Help me to never hesitate to share the gospel of Christ and His love with anyone who needs to hear it. Amen.

SELFIE 40

DECEMBER 27, 2020

MY SUNDAY BEST: I bet you're wondering why I'm wearing a fur hat inside? It can be chilly in Tulsa in January and since I would have worn this mink wraparound hat to in-person church service, I figured it would work for Sunday service on Zoom! By the way, this hat has matching cuffs accented with rhinestones. The cuffs are very versatile, and I can pair them with lots of different looks.

Order

As a child, I was a flighty little girl who was all over the place. So much so that my mother used to call me Helter Skelter. I was the quintessential tomboy who loved climbing trees and didn't mind getting dirty. I'd come into the house and drop my clothes anywhere and everywhere.

I didn't care anything about being dainty or organized. I was playful and just wanted to have fun.

But when I became an adult, something happened. I became a neatnik. My sister Jewell teases me about that because she remembers how I used to be. My home today

HALF MARATHON

La Verne Ford Wimberly
1st Place
Female 75 & Over
3:31:25

is well kept, and everything has its place. I even have an organizer for my tote bag with compartments so that I don't have to rummage through my things to find what I'm looking for. Helter Skelter transformed into Tidy La Verne. I don't know how or exactly when. But there is hope for the chaotic among us.

God certainly can bring order to confusion. That's why I pray that He orders my steps, especially before I take on challenges. At the age of seventy-seven, I decided to enter Tulsa's Route 66 Marathon and walk the 13.1-mile half marathon route. I was not sure if I could realize my dream of crossing the finish line, so I prayed that God would order my steps. He faithfully walked with me every step.

I completed a half marathon and finished first in my age group. I was so proud of myself and thanked the Lord for giving me the strength and courage to stay the course. Indeed, I can do all things through the One who orders my steps.

All along the way I recited statements to encourage myself:

I can do all things through Christ who strengthens me.
(Philippians 4:12–14 NKJV)

I am strong, I am fast, I am confident.

Doubt is not welcome today.

Walk far, walk strong.

This is my time to shine.

I believe I can, so I will.

Everything I need is within me, given to me by God.

My body is strong, my mind is stronger.

Giving it my all.

I will fly, I will finish.

Hallelujah, I did it!

Several years before, my friend Carolyn and I decided to enter the Tulsa Run race and walk together. Before the event began, Carolyn told me very emphatically that she did not want to talk during the race and would not be speaking to me. I told her fine, I also did not like talking to anyone while in pursuit of the finish line.

Little did Carolyn know that I was a speed racer in comparison to her. I left her in the dust. I didn't see her again until she crossed the finish line about twenty minutes after me. We would not have been able to talk even if we had wanted to. To make matters worse, Carolyn is a few years younger than I am. We still laugh about that today.

SELFIE 41
JANUARY 3, 2021

MY SUNDAY BEST: My husband and I were regulars at a Black-owned restaurant in Tulsa that had the best fried chicken! They really knew how to cook it to perfection: crispy on the outside and tender on the inside. The restaurateur always loved my hats, and one Christmas he bought me this one! I love the way it looks with my houndstooth suit.

Provision

My husband, James, really took to heart the adage, "A penny saved is a penny earned." I was always amused to hear him say we could become millionaires if only he had just a little help from me. Well, that didn't happen, although I did manage to curtail some of my frivolous spending as I grew older.

If I die penniless, I won't have any regrets. Like my mother, I just want to have enough money for someone to bury me. I had a colleague who retired and then died five days later. She didn't have a chance to draw even one retirement check. She pinched and saved all those years for what? Life is not promised to you. You have to grab hold of those golden rings and enjoy life while you can.

From experience I've learned a few things about money. I would encourage anyone entering the workforce to begin saving immediately. There are multiple benefits in saving, such as home ownership, early retirement, and financial independence. You will also have a financial cushion in case of job loss and unforeseen expenses.

If you want a good life in retirement, begin to save more than you spend. Pay yourself first after giving your tithes and offerings to the Lord. Always make a budget and try to stay within it.

Fortunately, I was able to begin saving soon enough to enjoy life after retirement. I could have done so much better. Still, no regrets!

Lord, thank You for Your provision. It all belongs to You, not me. Please help me to be a good steward of Your blessings. In Jesus' name. Amen.

Let your

DETERMINATION

to
succeed

OUT-

WEIGH

YOUR "I CAN'T."

SELFIE 42

JANUARY 10, 2021

MY SUNDAY BEST: It was still January. Still cold. How do you like my fur beret?

Resourcefulness

The heart of the discerning acquires knowledge,
for the ears of the wise seek it out.

—PROVERBS 18:15 NIV

God has blessed me with the gift of resourcefulness. I know how to obtain information and put people in place to do whatever job is at hand. And I am happy to be a resource for others.

One of my greatest successes is being able to identify people who can get the work done. I believe you need God-given discernment to do that. You can't know or do everything yourself. I'll be the first to admit I'm not a know-it-all. Only God knows everything. I'm never afraid to say, "I don't know," "I need help," or "Can you help me?" The Bible says, "Ask and it shall be given." Well, I certainly know how to ask—as well as to seek and find.

I've become adept at online research to look for information I need. In this age of googling and asking Alexa, I also know how to get information the old-fashioned way—looking it up at the library. I've been a member of the Tulsa City County Library Commission for more than a quarter of a century. We oversee twenty-four library branches and everything from expenditures to personnel. I've been reappointed by five mayors. So I am well acquainted with libraries and know how to use them.

Thanks to my father, numbers fascinate me. Dad had an amazing recall for figures. Likewise, I have a very good memory for dates. I can rattle off with ease birthdays, anniversaries, dates in history, and other personally significant days, such as the graduations and deaths of loved ones. My head for figures has come in handy. But that doesn't mean I'm especially good at math. That's a different beast and not my strength!

Beyond that, I try to be resourceful in other ways. During one Communion service at church, I struggled somewhat with opening the tiny, tightly sealed plastic container that held the bread and wine for the Lord's Supper. I told myself that I was not going to be defeated in my quest to partake in Communion in the future. After that incident, I started to carry a small pair of scissors in my purse that I use to open the elements. I've reduced my frustration level significantly. Necessity is indeed the mother of invention.

Thank You, Lord, for the ideas and skills You have given me to solve problems and effectively serve You. Amen.

MY SUNDAY BEST: I'm wearing the same outfit in a photo that hangs in the La Verne Ford Wimberly Media Center at my alma mater, Booker T. Washington High School. My hat is similar to a red hat I wore in Selfie 39.

Travel

My husband, James, didn't like to fly, and I didn't know that until after we married. I love to travel—I got that from my parents. Our first year as husband and wife I wanted us to fly to Miami to go on vacation. He told me he wasn't going. I thought that was strange, but as a newlywed I just let it go and didn't push it.

The next year I brought it up again and he still said we weren't going. I thought, *if he thinks I'm going to stay put and not fly, we might as well end this relationship now.*

I told him I was going to make the arrangements to go and if he wanted to come along, that would be fine. He didn't believe me. I made all the arrangements for us: I got airline tickets, the hotel, everything. I even packed our bags. Until the day we were to leave, he said he wasn't going. That morning I got ready to go and, to my surprise, he did too. He grumbled and carried on something terrible on the plane. But he enjoyed Florida. After that, for the first six years of our marriage, we compromised. We alternated the modes of transportation each year: we would fly one year for vacation, and the next year we would take a Greyhound or Continental Trailways bus tour. That's how we coexisted. Later, James got into cruising and the only way he could do that was to fly to get to the departure ports.

James used to love to tell his friends, "Man, I got a wife who does everything when we travel. I don't have to do anything. She makes the arrangements, packs my clothes, and tells me what to put on. I'm just like a little kid going somewhere with my mama."

Had I not put my foot down about traveling, we never would have enjoyed all the wonderful trips we had together. Sometimes you have to be very persistent—or at least be willing to compromise—to get what you want.

SELFIE 44

JANUARY 24, 2021

MY SUNDAY BEST: This wide-brimmed fur hat has feathers! I got it at a store in Utica Square in Tulsa. The store has gone out of business, and I'm so glad I bought this hat before it closed.

Sisterhood

I am a member of Alpha Kappa Alpha Sorority, Inc. AKA was founded in 1908 and is the oldest African American sorority. We now have more than 300,000 members internationally, including Vice President Kamala Harris, actor Phylicia Rashaad, writer Toni Morrison, Rev. Bernice King, and all three "Hidden Figures," computer pioneers Katherine Johnson, Mary Jackson, and Dorothy Vaughan. It is a joy that my sister Jewell is also a member. We belong to the same chapter and frequently attend events together. I was honored to serve as president of my Alpha Chi Omega chapter in 2008 for the centennial.

I belong to a sorority, but because God's love dwells richly inside me, every woman is my sister.

Etiquette

I'm big on etiquette. I attribute that to my mother and the classes we had at church that taught girls social graces and manners, and what a lady should and shouldn't do. Those lessons have stayed with me all my life.

Always say please and thank you.
Put your napkin in your lap.
Do not speak while chewing your food.
No elbows on the table.
Address people by their titles.
Do not address elders by their first names.
Always be well groomed.
Speak slowly and clearly.
Look people in the eye when you speak to them.

Those are just a few things I learned.

Trust

Trust in the LORD with all your heart
and lean not on your own understanding.

—PROVERBS 3:5 NIV

Things are bound to happen in life.

If you haven't experienced any hard times, just keep on living, as my grandmother used to say. That's when you have to put your trust in the Lord. I used to hear the old people sing a hymn called "Leaning on the Everlasting Arms" (written by A. J. Showalter in 1887, public domain). It starts off, "What a fellowship, what a joy divine, leaning on the everlasting arms; what a blessedness, what a peace is mine, leaning on the everlasting arms." I got tired of that song when I was younger. Now that I'm the "old people," I understand what it means to lean on the Lord and trust Him.

I've certainly had to trust God in my career to help me accomplish my goals. But I've also had to trust Him in other circumstances. Some were a little scary. I remember a return flight home from Germany. I was aboard a new luxury Lufthansa plane, and all was going well—until without warning we encountered air turbulence. The plane's speed suddenly dropped from nearly 600 mph to around 155 mph.

We bounced up and down for more than three hours before the pilot spoke to us—and then it was in German! I didn't understand a word he said. During that frightening time, I had to put my trust in God. James Cleveland's song "Peace Be Still" came to mind, so I kept reciting the lyrics. They were meaningful to me. Just as the disciples cried out to Jesus when they were afraid in the boat on the stormy seas, I did the same while on that plane in the unfriendly skies. Finally, a peace swept over me as my trust in God kicked in. I also repeated the King James Version of Isaiah 26:3: "Thou wilt keep him in perfect peace, whose mind is stayed on thee: because he trusteth in thee." It's important to know Scripture so that you can recall it at times like that.

The Lord never promised us a picnic in life. And I don't expect one. But I'm sure glad that my trust in Him is never misplaced and I can always lean on His everlasting arms.

Lord Jesus, I'm so glad that I can always trust You. Thank You for keeping me through thick and thin. In Your name I pray. Amen.

SELFIE 45

JANUARY 31, 2021

MY SUNDAY BEST: I just love this purple suit and the hat that's adorned with netting, rhinestones, satin, and lace applique. Purple symbolizes royalty, and I feel regal when I wear this suit.

Wimberly's Words of Wisdom

READING

can change YOUR LIFE.

MY SUNDAY BEST: I have a few black hats that are rather plain, so I enjoy adding a little something to make the hat pop! I adorned this hat with a black-and-white necklace.

Protection

"Be strong and courageous. Do not be
afraid or terrified because of them, for
the LORD your God goes with you; he will
never leave you nor forsake you."

—DEUTERONOMY 31:6 NIV

I feel God's protection every single day. When I'm driving and trying to get on the expressway with cars zooming by, I always ask the Lord to clear a path so that I can safely enter the roadway. And He does it every single time. I'm just amazed by that. Every day when I leave the house and return home safely, that's God. He is my protector.

*Thank You, Lord Jesus, for shielding me from
dangers seen and unseen. Amen.*

Do not regret

AGING and

GROWING OLD;

it is a **BLESSING**

denied to many.

SELFIE 47

FEBRUARY 14, 2021

MY SUNDAY BEST: This is one of my favorite hats. I just love the design! The color! The satin, the lace, and the rhinestones! Doesn't it look as if I'm wearing two hats? But it's only one! This fabulous hat really enhances my blue-and-black suit, piped with gold.

Hope

Mother

> But if we hope for what we do not yet
> have, we wait for it patiently.
>
> —ROMANS 8:25 NIV

You must have hope—something to live for, to build on, to motivate you. If you don't have goals or motivation, what keeps you going or propels you? Whatever your goal or vision, you can only accomplish it if you have hope and faith in God.

Even though my hope is in the Lord, there have been times that what I wanted and prayed for didn't happen. My greatest hope was that there would be a cure for ALS for my mother and that my father would walk again after his stroke. Mother wanted to live to be seventy; Psalm 90:10 says, "The days of our years are threescore years and ten" (KJV). She was happy to reach that mark and retired at seventy. But she passed away at seventy-three. I especially wanted Mother to live much longer. She had given so much of herself for so long to take care of my father, my sister, and me. But a longer life for her and healing for Dad were not in God's plan. Initially I was angry because I thought God hadn't heard my prayers. I was counting on Him to come through. I was able to overcome my anger, however, when I finally dug deep into the Word and understood that everything is according to His will, not mine.

My hope is that I will reach one hundred years old and still be able to live independently without any major health issues. I pray every night to God that He will let me live that long, but I always add "according to your will." I recognize that He is in charge, not me. I'm doing everything I can to prolong my life: exercise, eat right, and keep my mind active. Regardless of what happens, my hope remains in Him.

Dear Lord, may I always cling to my hope in You and remember that everything in this life is according to Your will. In Jesus' name I pray. Amen.

SELFIE 48

FEBRUARY 21, 2021

MY SUNDAY BEST: I love jewel tones, especially burgundy. It's one of my favorite colors and is featured prominently in my home (check out the wallpaper behind me). I was born in January and garnet is my birthstone, which is very close in color to burgundy! My hat has rhinestones and satin bows. (Have you noticed a theme?)

I thank my God every time I
remember you.

—PHILIPPIANS 1:3 NIV

SELFIE 49

FEBRUARY 28, 2021

MY SUNDAY BEST: I normally wear red during the Christmas holidays, Breast Cancer Awareness Month, or in February. This selfie was taken around Valentine's Day. The black hat with gold trim matches my suit nicely.

Honor

I am honored that people have thought enough of me and my service to recognize and remember me in a variety of ways. The media center/library at Tulsa's Booker T. Washington High School is named after me. I was part of the inaugural ten-person class selected for the Oklahoma African American Educators Hall of Fame. An artistic rendering of me is on the gymnasium wall at Carver Middle School, where I was once the principal. As a member of the Tulsa City-County Library Commission for more than twenty-five years, my name appears on the wall of various libraries. When I think that future generations will know and remember my name, I am overwhelmed and humbled.

SELFIE 50

MARCH 7, 2021

MY SUNDAY BEST: This is my favorite suit, and it also has a matching stole, pants, and skirt! It's very versatile, and I love the various looks that I can create. My hat is accented with rhinestones and satin.

Meditation

You can say that I have engaged in meditation since I was a kid. I was introduced to it by my parents. I was a mischievous child who often teased and annoyed my older sister. I recall one snowy winter evening when I was five years old, I was sitting with Jewell near a blazing stove, and I persuaded her to put her house slippers in the fire to see if they would burn. She did—and I was in big trouble. My parents had me sit alone for an extended period to think about what I had done and how I was going to behave going forward. That wasn't the first time for such punishment. I sat alone many times meditating on my misbehaving acts.

I am proud to say that, as I matured, I progressed from meditating on mischief to meditating on good things like God's Word. Philippians 4:8 says, "Finally, brothers and sisters, whatever is true, whatever is noble, whatever is right, whatever is pure, whatever is lovely, whatever is admirable—if anything is excellent or praiseworthy—think about such things" (NIV). Psalm 1:1–2 tells us, "Blessed is the one . . . whose delight is in the law of the Lord, and who meditates on his law day and night" (NIV).

You can't go wrong pondering and meditating on the Word. Sit and think about that.

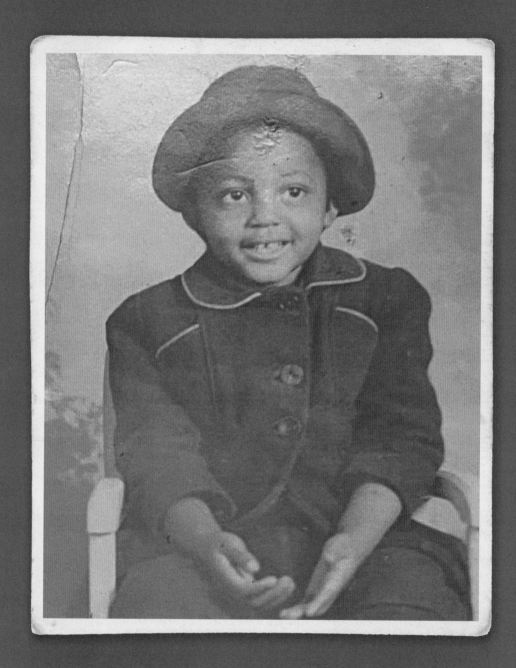

SELFIE 51

MARCH 14, 2021

MY SUNDAY BEST: This hat is the same style as my gray hat (Selfie 50). I have a few fuchsia hats, and this is another! I like the way the brooch and earrings pick up the colors in my suit. More jewel tones.

Victory

SELFIE 52

MARCH 21, 2021

CROWNING GLORY: This is a lovely green hat. I have lots of pink and green in my wardrobe because I'm a proud and devoted member of Alpha Kappa Alpha Sorority, Inc. Vice President Kamala Harris is also a member!

But thanks be to God, who gives us the victory through our Lord Jesus Christ.

—1 CORINTHIANS 15:57 ESV

For me, victory is all about completing the race you have set for yourself. You don't have to come in first. You just have to finish. I am reminded of 2 Timothy 4:7 in which the apostle Paul says, "I have fought the good fight, I have finished the race, I have kept the faith" (NKJV). That is what I am striving to do.

I have had many victories in my life. Against the odds, I earned three academic degrees. I rose through the ranks to become interim superintendent of Tulsa Public Schools, where I was once a student. When I was seventy-seven, I overcame my fear of dogs and cats to train outdoors so that I could walk a half-marathon. I stayed happily married to one man for forty-four years. I used to tease James by promising I'd give him fifty years of marriage. Each year I'd count down, and say something like, "I've given you forty years. Only ten more to go, then I'm out of here." He was the love of my life until the day he died. And I made it through a once-in-a-lifetime worldwide pandemic. I count all these things and more as victories and give God all the glory.

I plan to continue living with as much perseverance and stamina as I can. As I've mentioned, I want to live to be one hundred years old! That is why I'm so adamant and diligent about exercising—walking, lifting weights, and taking spinning classes at the health club with people about a quarter of my age—and keeping my mind active. Like the Energizer Bunny, I want to keep going. The grace that God has afforded me is amazing. I am living victoriously.

I consider myself a winner by all accounts because I know Jesus. I delight in the life I have. While I am thankful for my many successes, I also anticipate the utmost victory: everlasting life when my time on earth ceases. The final victory is entering eternal rest with the Lord.

Till then, I want
to finish strong.

Don't you?

Father God, thank You for the

multitude of blessings

You have so graciously bestowed

upon me. Most of all, thank You for

the promise of victory in Jesus

when I reach my heavenly home.

I praise Your holy name! Amen.

Ready for
the Word

Selfie Scriptures and Words of Inspiration

When I posted my first selfie on March 29, 2020, I never imagined the pandemic would last such a long time and that our church would have virtual services for one year! I just wanted to brighten the corner where I was by posting a photo and writing, "I'm ready for the Word, and I hope you are too!" As the weeks passed, I appreciated that people liked my hats and outfits, and dressing in my Sunday best for virtual church lifted my spirits and others, but I wanted to keep the focus on the most potent encouragement of all, the Word of God! So I started adding Scripture and some inspirational words in May and continued until March 21, 2021. Here's what I posted with my selfies:

May 3, 2020 Communion Sunday: Matthew 26:26–28

May 31, 2020 Relying on God's Word: Proverbs 3–5

June 7, 2020 Communion Sunday: Luke 22:17–19

June 14, 2020 Faith: Romans 10:17. The Word: Psalm 119:105

June 21, 2020 Hope in God's Word: Psalm 130:5

June 28, 2020 The Lord as Savior: Psalm 18:2

July 5, 2020 Communion Sunday: Mark 14:22–24

July 12, 2020 Spiritual Wisdom: Ephesians 1:17. Fear: Isaiah 41:10

July 19, 2020 Do Not Worry or Fear: Philippians 4:6–7

July 26, 2020 Living a Godly Life Through God's Word: John 6:63

August 2, 2020 Communion Sunday: 1 Corinthians 11:25–26. Fear: Proverbs 29:25 and Isaiah 35:4

August 9, 2020 Enrichment: 1 Corinthians 1:5. God's Protection: Deuteronomy 31:8

August 16, 2020 God's Word: Psalm 119:162

August 23. 2020 God's Love for Us and Hope: Romans 5:5, Proverbs 23:18. A Day of Rejoicing: Psalm 118:24

August 30, 2020 Charge to Be Holy: 1 Peter 1:15–16, Romans 12:2

September 6, 2020 Communion Sunday: Matthew 26:26–28. The Glory of Christ, 2 Corinthians 4:4

September 13, 2020 The Powerful Word of God: Hebrews 4:12

September 20, 2020 Reading Scripture and Capturing God's Word: Timothy 3:15–17

September 27, 2020 Having Peace in a Time of Storm: John 14:27

October 4, 2020 Communion Sunday: 1 Corinthians 11:23–26. Praying for All: 1 Timothy 2:1–3

October 11, 2020 It is More Blessed to Give than Receive: Acts 20:35, Proverbs, 3:27–28, and 2 Corinthians 9:7–9

October 18, 2020 God's Word as a Firm Foundation (Included the lyrics to the hymn "How Firm a Foundation")

October 25, 2020 Going with the Strength You Have with God; Judges 6:14–16

November 1, 2020 Communion Sunday: Luke 22:17–20. Walking with the Lord: Genesis 5:24, Genesis 6:9, and Micah 6:8

November 8, 2020 Not Being Afraid: 2 Chronicles 20:15–17. Perfect Peace: Isaiah 26:3. Finding New Strength: Isaiah 40:31. Being Patient in Trouble: Romans 12:12. Waiting Patiently: Psalm 37:7, Psalm 62:1–2, Psalm 27:13–14. Counting on the Lord: Psalm 130:5

November 15, 2020 Growing your Faith: Matthew 13:1–9, Mark 4:1–20, and Luke 8:4–15

November 22, 2020 Giving Thanks and Being Joyful: 1 Thessalonians 5:16

November 29, 2020 Listening to God, James 1:22–25, Mark 4:24–25. First Sunday of Advent (Hope)

December 6, 2020 Communion Sunday: Mark 14:22–24. The Story of Jesus: Luke 1:26–35, Luke 2:1–7. Second Sunday of Advent (Peace).

December 13. 2020 The Joy of Christmas: Micah 5:2. Third Sunday of Advent (Joy)

December 20, 2020 Fourth Sunday of Advent (Love): Matthew 1:18–21, John 3:16

December 27, 2020 The Word of God: Isaiah 40:8. Looking Ahead: Isaiah 43:18–19, Philippians 3:13–14

January 3, 2021 Communion Sunday: Luke 17-20. God's Faithfulness: Lamentations 3:22–23. Thanks for Making All Things New: Psalm 65:11

January 10, 2021 Nourishment from God's Word: Proverbs 2:6. God's Peace: Philippians 4:8–9

January 17, 2021 God's Unfailing Love: Psalm 57:10, Psalm 69:16, and 1 John 4:7

January 24, 2021 Renewing Your Mind: Romans 12:2. Growing Older: Psalm 92:12–15

January 31, 2021   Holiness: John 17:17. Age and Wisdom: Job 12:12. Praising God for Old Age: Psalm 71:7–9, 17–18

February 7, 2021   Communion Sunday: 1 Corinthians 11:23–29. When Trouble Comes: James 1:2–8

February 14, 2021   Enduring Word of God: 1 Peter 1:25, John 15:7, and Psalm 91:1. Beginning of Lent: A time of self-examination, spiritual discipline/renewal, and reflection on Jesus.

February 21, 2021   Believing and Meditating on God's Word: 1 Thessalonians 2:13, Romans 10:17, Psalm 77:11–12, Psalm 63:6, and Psalm 143:5. The Lenten season is a time to praise and worship the Lord, read the Scriptures more often, pray more often, and meditate on God's Word more often.

February 28, 2021   God's Divinity: John 1:14, Colossians 2:9, Psalm 86:11, and Psalm 1:2

March 7, 2021   Communion Sunday: Matthew 26:26–28. Taking Refuge in God: Proverbs 30:5. Spirit and Life: John 6:63. God's Word Bears Fruit: Isaiah 55:11. Finding Strength in God's Word: Philippians 4:19

March 14, 2021   The Faithfulness of God: Psalm 33:4. Rejoicing in the Lord: Psalm 104:34

March 21, 2021   Good morning, Metropolitan Baptist Church Family! Today is the fifty-second Sunday we've had virtual church. Can you believe that a whole year has passed since we worshiped together as a body in the sanctuary? Your favorable responses to my Sunday Selfies kept me writing for fifty-two Sundays. I believe we'll return to church soon, so there's no longer a need for me to continue the weekly communications. Nevertheless, I am ready for the Word, and I hope you are too! God's Word is True: 2 Samuel 7:28, Psalm 119:43! There can be no better way to end these Sunday Facebook postings than to remember the importance of Easter. The importance of Easter is to praise and acknowledge Jesus Christ's resurrection from the dead and His glorious assurance of eternal life for all who believe in Him. Holy Week commemorates Jesus' triumphal entry into Jerusalem, an event chronicled in Matthew, Mark, Luke, and John. Next Sunday is Palm Sunday, also called Passion Sunday, in the Christian tradition. It marks the first day of Holy Week and the Sunday before Easter. Jesus journeyed to Jerusalem, knowing He would be tried and crucified. For God so Loved the World: John 3:16 and Jesus as the Resurrection and the Life: John 11:25.

NOTE: I always concluded each post by mentioning COVID-19. I reminded everyone to wear a mask, wash their hands frequently, practice social distancing, and pray for those affected. I also reminded people to remember to pay their tithes and offerings.

Acknowledgments

First and foremost, all praises and thanks to our Lord and Savior for favoring me with a multitude of blessings during 2020–2022 that changed my life immensely for the better!

Thanks to Kimberly Jackson Hilliard, KTUL (Channel 8), a TV reporter who did the first story about me dressing in my Sunday best for virtual church services during the first year of Covid-19. The story went viral thanks to Cathy Free's *Washington Post* article that appeared on the front page on Easter Sunday 2021. These two ladies provided me moments of fame that I'll treasure forever.

I am indebted to my editor, Janet Talbert, who with a healthy assist from her husband, Aaron, tracked me down through my church and suggested that I had a story to tell and should consider writing a book.

My thanks and appreciation to Robin Watkins, Metropolitan Baptist Church clerk, who was saddled with the task of answering the many calls and responding to messages from people (including those Talberts!) who wanted to communicate with me in the wake of the media explosion that was set off by the *Washington Post* article.

I am in awe of Barbranda Walls, the writer who was able to tell my story in such a colorful, factual, and captivating way. I'm ever grateful. Kudos.

My sincere thanks to my agent, Marie Brown, who stepped in to close the deal, and the team at Nelson Books: Janet, Janene, Emily, John, Sarah, Lisa, Andrew, Kathryn, Debbie, Meg, Jamekra, everyone in sales, and anyone else who helped make this book a reality.

My thanks to the Tulsa City–County Library staff: Kimberly Johnson, John Fancher, Rebekah Cowan, and Allison Embry for their willingness to help with photography, technology, research, and marketing. There's a photo of me on page 87 that was taken by Turner Goodrum several years ago. Thanks, Turner, for making me look like a starlet.

Thanks so much to everyone at the Greenwood Cultural Center. Special thanks to Frances Jordan and Michelle Burdex for helping with the Black Wall Street photos.

My profound gratitude to my family: Jewell and Marvin Maynard, Marva and Darren Walter, Stephen and Francyenne Maynard, Don and Linda Wofford, Patricia Rhymes, Altricia and Carl Foster, William Ford, Donn L. Latimer, Dianne Conage, Donna and Booker Washington, Mark and Rhonda Wimberly, and Ruthie Wheatley who encouraged me to take the leap of faith and say "yes" to writing the book.

Special thanks to my friends: Bobbie Allen Booker, Marilyn Britton Mayes, and Carolyn White who assured me I had a delightful story to tell and could do it.

My heartfelt thanks and gratitude to all!

About the Author

Dr. La Verne Ford Wimberly is a retired career educator who played a role in desegregating the Tulsa school system. She later became the first interim African American female superintendent and has a trail of honors in her wake. Dr. Wimberly was most recently the chairperson of the Greenwood Cultural Center Board of Directors and the chair of the Board of Trustees at her beloved Metropolitan Baptist Church. The library at her alma mater, Booker T. Washington High School, is named after Dr. Wimberly and there are murals of her in schools throughout Tulsa. Plus, there are two days in the year that Tulsa declared "Dr. La Verne Ford Wimberly Day"; and that was all before she posted her first Sunday Best selfie!

Dr. Wimberly lives in Tulsa, Oklahoma, and is a member of Alpha Kappa Alpha, Inc., the oldest and largest African American sorority.